learning to be
in the world
with others

We will get
through this....
aces o winners, days.

Studies in Criticality

Shirley R. Steinberg
General Editor

Vol. 506

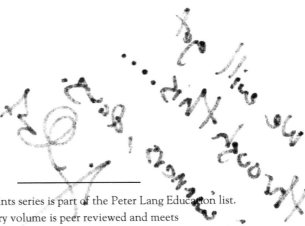

The Counterpoints series is part of the Peter Lang Education list.
Every volume is peer reviewed and meets
the highest quality standards for content and production.

PETER LANG
New York • Bern • Frankfurt • Berlin
Brussels • Vienna • Oxford • Warsaw

H. James Garrett

learning to be
in the world
with others

difficult knowledge & social studies education

PETER LANG
New York • Bern • Frankfurt • Berlin
Brussels • Vienna • Oxford • Warsaw

Library of Congress Cataloging-in-Publication Data
Names: Garrett, H. James, author.
Title: Learning to be in the world with others: difficult knowledge
and social studies education / H. James Garrett.
Description: New York: Peter Lang, 2017.
Series: Counterpoints: studies in criticality; v. 506 | ISSN 1058-1634
Includes bibliographical references and index.
Identifiers: LCCN 2016036399 | ISBN 978-1-4331-3238-4 (hardcover: alk. paper)
ISBN 978-1-4331-3237-7 (paperback: alk. paper) | 978-1-4331-3966-6 (ebook pdf)
ISBN 978-1-4331-3967-3 (epub) | ISBN 978-1-4331-3968-0 (mobi)
Subjects: LCSH: Social sciences—Study and teaching.
Social science teachers—Training of. | Reflective teaching. | Self-culture.
Classification: LCC LB1584 .G34 2017 | DDC 300.71—dc23
LC record available at https://lccn.loc.gov/2016036399
DOI 10.3726/978-1-4331-3966-6

Bibliographic information published by **Die Deutsche Nationalbibliothek**.
Die Deutsche Nationalbibliothek lists this publication in the "Deutsche
Nationalbibliografie"; detailed bibliographic data are available
on the Internet at http://dnb.d-nb.de/.

The paper in this book meets the guidelines for permanence and durability
of the Committee on Production Guidelines for Book Longevity
of the Council of Library Resources.

Printed in the United States of America

TABLE OF CONTENTS

PREFACE

I was sitting in my office, late in the fall of 2012, on the campus of the University of Georgia meeting with a doctoral student. Following that conversation I was to meet my wife and my three children—at that time ages 4, 2, and eight months old—for lunch. It was my wife's 33rd birthday.

My phone rang. I saw that it was my wife calling and when I answered it she told me that she had been diagnosed with breast cancer. She told me where she was and she told me to come there, and, of course, what she told me was much more than anyone can make sense of. In such moments, I think, lives likely change forever. Mine did. I had been studying difficult knowledge and psychoanalysis for several years by this point, but the distance from trauma in my personal life had been up until then a remarkably safe one. Neither my experience nor my education gave me anything by way of tools to now understand and move through my own crisis of education (learning now about how to live) as I drove to meet my wife and children at that playground near my office where we sometimes still go and where that memory comes jarringly back. My children were eating a bag of M&M's, sharing them amongst themselves, a tool of distraction so she and I could look at each other and see if we could figure out who we now were, somehow looking at each other in immediacy and terror, longing for it to be a dream.

The turmoil of crisis is immediate. When I drove the children through the drive-through at McDonald's they were so happy. To have a treat. This was on our way back home. And my despair grew by the moment. I spoke to my father-in-law. "Not good," he said, choking back tears. "No. Not good," I said. The kinds of questions we had were the worst kind. I recall sitting with social workers who spoke with us about moving forward through diagnosis, and I recall my wife talking about how this very thing was kind of like what I studied for my work. I clutched a box of tissues.

My wife, Logan, was turning 33 the day she was diagnosed with breast cancer. This is a trauma, something that

> can never be let go of: it holds you. It locates you at the knot that joins the personal and the impersonal, specifying you at the moment you have the least control over your own destiny and meaning. You become like a small animal that, when picked up, never stops moving its legs. (Berlant, 2011, p. 127)

The week became a long lesson plan. But the trauma. Which is it? Is it the cancer? It was already there. It had been for some time. No, she did not catch it early. Yes, it was large. Yes, she needed chemotherapy. Yes, she needed to have a mastectomy. Yes, it was treatable. And yes, she would be fine, they all would say.

But more immediately: Yes, our baby needed to stop breastfeeding. And so began the darkest nights of my life. Alone with our youngest daughter, robbed of her favorite thing in the whole world, the thing that soothed and provided her with what she needed to live. And so we had each other to find, because to be with her mother but without feeding would have been even more unbearable for both of them. We cried together, likely for each other and for her mother, and worked together to understand how to go on. I was a specified me. So the trauma wasn't the cancer, then, the trauma was the diagnosis and the knowledge about the world and what is important in it that came after. New knowledge was on the scene and had collapsed the stage right under us. This is an intimate example of difficult knowledge.

Berlant writes with unconceivable precision about such times of living in crisis. She writes that "to be in crisis is not to have the privilege of the taken-for-granted: it is to bear an extended burden of vulnerability for an undetermined duration" (p. 62). Such an extended vulnerability moves my story into the present, three years cancer free, Logan and I are haunted with the ghosts of what might be. Even typing this sentence presses upon me that by the time of publication, or the time of any reading, these sentences (or any) may not any longer be true. Life is fragile, we all know that but I learned it at that time, after an almost unbelievably crisis-free life to that point. I understood that as a privilege, one I got to hold onto longer than most, but one that I wouldn't wish for anyone to check. We all know that this is a privilege that will be checked sooner or later. And I learned, too, that there is a kind of good news that can be so good that it will make you sit down and weep wherever you are. That I hadn't learned these things before is a loud reminder of my own privilege and made me recognize how many others confront such terrors much more incessantly and without any of the hope and resolution that I have.

It would make sense in the wake of my own personal crisis that my work, my research about difficult knowledge, took more urgency. It didn't, though. Living in and through the difficulties that knowledge brings also helps me realize the difficulties of knowledge also enable a living on. In a very immediate way, the pedagogical dimension of the relationship between knowing and living pressed upon me evidence of the importance of continued vigilant thinking about the relation between what we want to know and what it is that we will know; and what this knowledge will mean when we move in relationship to the world around us.

It is not as though there were much space between the personal reeling and the concretely political and civic issues that impacted Logan's journey through cancer treatment. Yes, this is my own story, but we were embedded in politics sitting in the waiting room. Astronomical health care prices made me even more dizzy than I was already. Hearing Logan tell me about the person with whom she spoke at every chemotherapy treatment who did not have health care coverage bewildered me from the beginning of the thought. Dealing with the terrors of a health crisis is awful. That it should be confounded and further complicated by a legislated inequity between people who have a particular kind of employment and those who do not is a brutal reality of a shortsighted public. Further, the ways in which the nation-state funds university research in an age of austerity should concern all of us. Taxes are viewed with such disdain that we withhold public money from the institutions that have provided our social fabric with the kinds of breakthroughs that allow us so much of our health and happiness. Research funding is cut. Should any reader think that these connections are being made simply in order to make an argument, I can only state that the simultaneity of the horror of my own situation and the horror at our collective disconnections to the ways our actions in the world yield a scenario that is willfully set against good health of our citizenry. These are stirred emotions that are elicited in making a relationship to difficult knowledge; the immediacy of the moment, the simultaneity of the intimate and the social.

In his introductory chapter to *Disavowed Knowledge* Peter Taubman (2012) writes that "all too often those who write about education and psychoanalysis ignore their own psychic investments and autobiographically overdetermined involvement in their work, but as psychoanalysis insists, those investments, one's family, and the intimate dead, however irrelevant they may seem to one's scholarship, are always pressing close" (p. 3). My own autobiographical conditions are closely connected to the work in this book and, thus, may provide a generative context for its presentation. I am intimately invested in exploring the ways in which learners may be invited into confrontation with their own views of the world, ways in which the social conditions may be revised to make things a bit less precarious for unknown others through revisions to our social/political policies. But in these last years my family and I have been presented with conditions that have seen us in terrifyingly close proximity to our shared precariousness. My wife's breast cancer diagnosis laid bare the reality that all of us live precarious lives. I dealt with that crisis by keeping things small because as Kevin Burke said to me on the phone one morning during all of this, the big things are too big.

But that task of keeping things small took creativity in the attempt to not be overwhelmed, and here is where my personal experience collapses into the preoccupations I have in research. Difficult knowledge denotes, for me, a particular relation to pedagogy and is a term that helps stand in for the ways in which what we do not want to know, or what we already know but have set aside, comes to have a tumultuous present. In the chapters that follow, those that were written before, during, and after this tumultuous year, I present difficult knowledge as an idea that stands in for the tense relation between questions we never want to ask and answers that challenge our ability to listen.

References

Berlant, L. G. (2011). *Cruel optimism*. Durham, NC: Duke University Press.

Taubman, P. M. (2012). *Disavowed knowledge: Psychoanalysis, education, and teaching*. New York, NY: Routledge.

ACKNOWLEDGMENTS

I first wish to acknowledge and express gratitude for Deborah Britzman's insistence on the psychical stakes of learning and teaching which has been such a productive influence in education. Her ideas are all over this book. Difficult knowledge, of course, is a term she first used and with it has provided many people a rich concept to think with. Her writing is what invited me to engage with psychoanalysis, her conceptual framework is what drives my research, and her support of my own work has been humbling. She was generous enough to meet with me while I was first writing with these ideas, told me to read my data like a novel, and has discussed ideas with me since then. I am tremendously thankful.

Avner Segall introduced me to Deborah Britzman and her work. As my doctoral advisor he supported my early engagements with psychoanalysis and difficult knowledge, but always challenged me to connect those engagements with the social studies. His commitments to, and critiques of, the field of social studies aid in its liveliness.

Karyn Sandlos, Sara Matthews, and Brian Casemore provide such thoughtful engagements with the complicated terrain of learning in their own work and have been extraordinarily generous with their intellect in conversations with me over the years. I would not be able engage with the ideas about which I try to work in this book without them. Karyn read and provided feedback that was critical to the development of several aspects of this book. Sandra Schmidt has provided continued support to me in various ways since before I even began thinking about life as an academic. Sandra read and offered generous and critical feedback on drafts of portions of this book as well.

I am indebted to my family. My parents and my sister never questioned my educational pursuits. My smart, engaged, inquisitive, energetic children—Ellis, Gretta, and Jolie—help me learn every day. I have the most supportive partner I can imagine; Logan's generosity and full-hearted engagement in life provide a model and lesson for me and for so many others who know her.

PERMISSIONS

An earlier version of chapter 4 appeared as "Routing and rerouting of difficult knowledge: Social studies teachers encounter *When the Levees Broke*" in *Theory and Research in Social Education*, 39 (3), 320–347. Reprinted with permission from Taylor & Francis.

An earlier version of chapter 5 appeared as "'This is the kind of hard that knows': Past, presence, and pedagogy in Toni Morrison's *Beloved*" in *The Journal of Curriculum and Pedagogy*, 15(1), 36–52. Reprinted with permission from Taylor & Francis.

Parts of chapter 6 appeared as "Why didn't I know this before?: Psychoanalysis, social studies education and *The Shock Doctrine*" in *Canadian Journal for Social Studies Education*. 45(2), 1–12. Reprinted with permission from the publisher.

· 1 ·

INTRODUCTION

Difficult Knowledge, Psychoanalysis, and Social Studies Education

As often as not, the knowledge we encounter in the world can make us want to not-know, turn away, accuse, correct, and forget. This book is meant to address the dynamics of learning when learning is experienced as a burden. I am interested in the energetic reactions inherent in such learning as well as the potential affordances of being able to trace those movements in pedagogy. These engagements with knowledge are particularly important in social studies education, the purpose of which is democratic practice. Democratic practices are predicated upon answers to the question of how we are going to be with others in the world.

How is this learned? Who are we? Who are these others? The others with whom we engage on a daily basis are those with whom we share physical space—our friends, teachers, parents, children, co-workers. They are also the servers and clerks who help us on our way. They are also the other drivers on the road who stay in their lane. However, we will likely never meet many of those with whom we act in concrete, though perhaps not self-evident, ways. What I mean is that we "act with" the people who make our smartphones and computers and tablets and clothes. We "act with" the farmers and truckers and workers as they make food available to us. We are sharing material with those thousands of miles away, with whom we likely will never stand face to face, who put together the machines with which we write and who stitch the fabric of the clothes we wear. Being in the world with others takes those others as simultaneously within our physical spaces and beyond them. Such a view requires that we investigate those seemingly vague connections, how "their" choices and "ours" are part of the same circuit of global capital, how historical processes have positioned people within networks that make large groups of people comfortable and have unfortunately positioned others as expendable and in the most callous instances systemically murdered them. There are lessons to be learned in all of these situations. There are also lessons to be learned in violent upheaval about the ways some people resist and provide shelter. There are lessons to be learned about how we relate to one another and how what we do is, even if it feels in its totality a 'private' affair, that it will likely carry (at least) a trace of social significance. Social studies education should help students engage with questions about what that could mean for them. This is no small task for a number of reasons.

Among these is the situation of formal education more broadly. If formal education is to hold any promise, I suspect that the promise has something to do with the processes of emergence of thought, revision rather than provision of knowledge, and reconsiderations of the self, the other, and the relationships between the two. In wider discussions of education and teaching, very little formal or systemic attention seems to be given over to such a position on knowledge. Instead, the force of socio-political discourses will make possible—and indeed forcefully encourage—other conversations, ones that are more about the steady transfer of knowledge and skills from the teacher (envisioned as a dispassionate expert of content and pedagogy) to the student (envisioned as future worker in a globalized economy or something like that). That structure has a profound influence on the spaces I occupy as a teacher and teacher-educator. Not only does the force of that structure put designs on what I would do in the university spaces, but it colors in the students' perceptual field of what they see and say in classrooms; it gives a certain striation to the careers being readied, and it physically adorns the walls of the classrooms into which they are placed.

Much of this is old news: Standards and accountability, their deep overestimation of the reach of "evidence based research," the over-investment in certainty and static lessons has been met with firm, loud, and enriching critique and resistance. I do not profess to have any idea about how this saga will morph into its "next" iteration. But I do know that the soon-to-be teachers with whom I work are worried. If learning to teach was not worrying enough, now it comes with the additional burden of surveillance, quantification and evaluation. Yet we carry on. We make lives in classrooms.

Another one of the difficulties of helping students into thinking about the questions of belonging in the world has to do with the more specific traditions of social studies education that are amplified and now validated and solidified through disciplinary focus. The sorts of disciplinary inquiry that are underwritten and encouraged by the C3 framework places the focus on the process that leads to something (college and career, notably) in the future (NCSS, 2013). Why not, I wonder, focus on the ways that civic readiness is something that is already important in the here-and-now situations in which people find themselves? The field stands as a disciplinary space that is dedicated to the development of productive and informed citizens yet in its official statements and in much of the scholarship in social studies, it neglects the social field of enacted practice, the very places and experiences of those undergoing the education.

Werner's (2000) articulation of social studies locates the field in the present tense as well, as he describes social education as "helping students acquire rich conceptual tools for thoughtfully reading their cultural world and acting within it" (p. 195). I begin here for what this statement of purpose does not say. To wit, it does not name the disciplines of history, economics, government and geography. It does not mention citizenship. It does not move the temporal horizon into a place other than the classroom. Rather, it emphasizes the possession ("their social world") of the social world by the learner and therefore reverses the traditional focus on the teacher's knowledge. Werner also formalizes the focus on action by utilizing the verbs acquire, read, and act. Knowledge here is used for something other than exchange; it is about being able to critically read the world and do something within it. As I articulate my version and vision for social education, I also feel compelled to move away from the disciplines that traditionally constitute the field. I recognize social education as that which might invite a learner into understanding the self, the Other, and the relationship between the two. In no way am I disavowing the intellectual histories and strategies for inquiry that are carried out by the disciplines. At the same time, I remain suspicious of what their separateness conceals for students and guess that the reason why something like neoliberalism is difficult to understand is because of the seeming separateness of post-WWII nation-states and their economies, something that I explore in chapter six.

After all, who is social studies education for? The students who are learning in our classrooms, born at the beginning of the twenty-first century, are living in unprecedented circumstances. They are being raised in an era of economic uncertainty, political stagnation, ubiquitous surveillance, hyper-mediation of information, continuous war, and looming environmental ca-tastrophe. These are unprecedented conditions of citizenship and require, I think, approaches that build upon the valuable work being done in social studies education. Learning about these ideas, as well as the ways in which people have consciously committed atrocious acts of violence, can bewilder the teacher and the student in the face of their seeming incomprehensibility.

Difficult Knowledge

This is a book that is in many ways a prolonged engagement, from within and directed toward, social studies education, with Britzman's (2000) question: "If teacher education could begin to reclaim difficult knowledge, what would be the work of teacher educators?" (p. 201) Difficult knowledge as a specific term in education research emerged through the work of Britzman (1998, 2000, 2003b, 2013) and Pitt & Britzman (2003) to "signify the teacher and students encounter with the painful and traumatic curriculum that represents history as the woeful disregard for the fragility of human life while seeking to cre-ate new meanings from the ravages of humanly induced suffering" (Britzman, 2013, p. 100). Related issues of pedagogy and trauma have been explored by others including Roger Simon (2005, 2014), Megan Boler (2004), Lisa Far-ley (2009), Aparna Tarc (2011, 2013), and Michalinos Zembylas (2014) to constitute lines of inquiry concerned with the pedagogical troubles associated with teaching a particular kind of content. Inquiries into difficult knowledge have demonstrated that learning about social upheaval, violence, loss, and suffering carries with it the potential to affect the pedagogical situation in surprising and tumultuous ways. Learners and teachers are pitched into their own crises as they encounter, perhaps unconsciously, their own experiences with loss, helplessness, and vulnerability.

However, the story of difficult knowledge is not bound solely within the terrain of learning about and from social/historical calamity. Difficult knowl-edge is also the "traces in narratives about knowledge" that resist narration and signal "a trauma in the very capacity to know" (Pitt & Britzman, 2003, p. 757). Difficult knowledge also asks the question about how we come to terms encounters that unsettle us to the core and demand that we tell new stories about the world, or asked differently, "what one makes from the ruins of one's 'lovely knowledge' (p. 766). And indeed, Britzman's (2013) own inquiry into this problematic space shifted from that particular focus on terrible human histories toward an inquiry "questioning the work of changing the mind through attention to the difficulties in symbolizing affect...affected by the group psychology of education" (p. 100). What this means is that difficult knowledge points attention to the dilemmas inherent in learning about upheaval but is also an acknowledgment of the radical uncertainty and ambiguity of what it means to learn to be with others in the world.

In this book I will take both vantages of difficult knowledge: that which focuses on the historical atrocities and the troubles those make for pedagogy and also that which considers the very problems of symbolizing affect as difficult knowledge. Although social studies educators may most immediately see the implications for the former, I will also discuss how the latter is significant for the field of inquiry and pedagogy concerned with how people consider and conceptualize their social lives. There are troubles associated with knowledge and learning. Sometimes we learn things that we do not want to know. Difficult knowledge is a pedagogical situation that is enlivened within contexts of tangled timelines (past, present, and future are interwoven) and the complications of human relations.

Teacher Education and Changing Your Mind

While I consider social studies to be the disciplinary domain with which I'm most familiar, I also think in terms of teacher education more broadly. Teacher education, though hardly a research site of the avant-garde, is a worthy case example of the spaces of formal pedagogy due to the ways in which the participants in that scene are regimented in particular ways toward the work that they think they are doing (Lortie, 1975; Britzman, 2003a). There are few other pedagogical locations in which those tasked with learning feel so familiar with and competent about what the learning will be before the learning begins (Britzman, 2012). Students becoming teachers have often been shown to demonstrate a perceived knowledge of their work in advance of their training. They know what it means to teach and think about learning before they take their first course. They carry with them the impressions and fantasies of their own school life and, wittingly or not, work to replay or re-do their own histories of schooling. They resist the lessons of their teacher education. Britzman (2009) puts it this way: "Everyone hates their own teacher education" (p. 38).

Perhaps this is what happens when someone is confronted with the necessity to change their minds. But changing someone's mind is exceedingly difficult, a problem I elaborate on in chapter three. As Alcorn (2013) writes in his exploration of how rational thinking without a consideration of the emotional stakes of learning will so often terribly fail to accommodate overwhelming factual evidence, "We seem unable to face the facts about our inability to take in facts" (p. 23). And so instead of a pedagogical situation in which we imagine teaching to be a transfer of knowledge, we might imagine classrooms that can attend to the simultaneous fragility of the self and the world as well as to the well-fortified structures put in place unconsciously to defend against acknowledging that fragility. This means more than putting our faith into experiential knowledge, clinical experiences, high-leverage practices, or performance assessments. To the point, it means that classrooms are acknowledged as places that will always defy our best wishes for certainty.

For social studies education and teacher education, rigid certainty ought to be considered as a worrisome concept indeed. In social studies education the goals (though contested) coalesce around the ideas of equality, "good" citizenship, and the health of democracy. Democracy involves the recognition of difference and an ability to withstand difference while acknowledging its difference. That requires a great deal of thought. The dangerous part of rigid certainty is that it actually requires us to "not think." If I am to know something (the right teaching method, for instance) for certain, then I am required to not think about the possibility of other courses of action being defensible and perhaps even being wonderful. This is why rigid certainty is better off resisted and problematized with particular attention to the social studies; citizens who are discouraged from thinking are likely to make poor choices about public policy and the people who represent their interests in office.

There is a benefit to thinking about the origins of our wishes for a list of best practices, just as there is benefit to acknowledging the impossibility of their existence. That benefit lies in the connections between the socially available and predominating ways of knowing and how deeply personal those ways of knowing feel to us. This is a pedagogical project of acknowledging that learning takes place within a psychical economy. It might begin with a confrontation of the realities of sustained aggression and injustice. That can be traumatic.

Psychoanalysis

My views of social studies and the concept of difficult knowledge are informed by psychoanalytic theory. Psychoanalysis first caught my attention as an undergraduate student. After encountering psychoanalytic models of personality in introduction to psychology courses, I used the ideas of oedipal conflict and repressed desire in my attempts to critique literature in English classes. I found these frames of understanding literature as interesting tools to accompany the more straightforward readings to which I was accustomed. But I was training to be a social studies teacher with an English minor, and so beyond those courses and those papers, I pretty much forgot psychoanalysis.

I then entered the teaching profession as a high school social studies teacher and my energies were fixated on critical media literacy. I had been exposed to this idea at a social studies conference and was immediately taken with ideas about representation, power, and ideology. I was excited by the idea that students could be invited into cultural critique through the very texts that they already enjoyed: popular film, reality television, music videos, and magazines. Around the same time, I was introduced to critical pedagogy. I was powerfully attracted to cultural reproduction and ideology critique. I found that infusing my teaching and my participation as a faculty member with these emerging critical sensibilities was necessary and ultimately "good" work.

I attempted to engage high school students with issues of structural injustice, racism, and issues of sexuality and socio-economic inequity. I constructed a course in which students created documentary films investigating the ways those big issues were present within the context of the school. The films were objects of deep investment for me and for many of the students. They were screened in front of large numbers of students, teachers, and administrators. There were widely mixed reactions. Among some of the students, teachers, and administrators were people who thought my teaching was irresponsible and dangerous; they thought I was advocating dangerous behaviors. They worried about the knowledge that was being represented in film.

I understand now that I was teaching angrily. I desperately wanted students to understand those issues. I wanted them to be concerned about them, too. Or, maybe I wanted them to have the same concerns as I had, forgetting our differences. But the students (who were mostly middle- and upper-middle-class white kids) reacted in ways that surprised me. They were angry. But they weren't angry because of some social injustice we were investigating in class. They were angry with me. They made jokes about injustice. Some students, of course, identified and took up some of critical vocabularies I was offering and were able to see the ways that issues of sexuality, race, class, and gender as broad social categories played out and took shape in their lives in schools. There were powerful testimonials to life in this particular high school. This was deeply satisfying. Other students, however, ignored and dismissed these as having any hold on the truth of their worlds. The different reactions to my pedagogy on the part of the students with whom I worked are part what led me to pursue doctoral work. I wanted strategies that could overcome those resistances in the students. I wanted them to be able to think the way I thought.

As my doctoral work progressed, what I began to understand is that my interest in media studies was less about media and more about the ways that knowledge (about the world, about ourselves, and the connections between the two) is always mediated. There is always something that stands in between object and understanding. When I borrowed Deborah Britzman's (2003b) *After-Education* from Avner Segall, my doctoral advisor, that intuition of mediated knowledge was enriched by the psychoanalytic vocabularies offering the structures and vagaries of the unconscious as being a primary mediator of knowledge. This began a momentous shift in my thinking. By using with the idea of education as a site of conflict, ambivalence, desire, and the unconscious I began to recognize my teaching was a defense against hearing students' ideas. I began to see that their resistance was not a problem to be overcome. Rather, their resistance was their first way of engaging with, rather than running from, the content. In this book, the pulls of engagement and disengagement are shown to be present in the encounters with difficult knowledge.

Psychoanalytic ideas. The unconscious began to signify for me a place of inquiry where I could acknowledge the sorts of multi-directional confusion and overabundance of reactions to the classrooms spaces I occupied as a student and as a teacher. I began to leave the popular culture version of the unconscious behind—the one where there is an internal puppet master pulling the strings—and became comfortable with a model of subjectivity in which the subject is defended, split, and working to protect itself from discomfort while always trying to satisfy desire.

Briefly, the unconscious is not as much of a "thing" but rather a set of processes that are always in relation to some other or others. In fact, Lacan (1998) defines the unconscious as "the discourse of the Other" (p. 131). What he signals here is that the unconscious is a social relation where the divisions, splits, and tensions are a result of the conflicts between expectations of society and the individual desire. And so the subject is the result of processes that accommodate those tensions.

One of those processes that has vital importance for education is transference, the idea that patterns from our first relationships are replayed and used as a kind of playbook for our later relationships. Lacan (1998) formulates transference occurring as anytime there is a "subject presumed to know." The "subject presumed to know" is more often than not the analyst, of course. It is the analyst, the "subject presumed to know," from whom we might want to demand answers, or plans of actions, or solutions to our problems. In psychoanalysis, unlike other forms of talk therapy, the doctor does not give the patient any strategies or advice. In analysis the focus is placed on the need for answers, what the questions reveal about what we want and what we fear, and on extending the inquiry rather than foreclosing it.

The ways we find ourselves demanding answers from a particular person are clues about the nature of our questions and the nature of our relationships. For a classroom, then, I began to understand the demand for authority as not only students' wanting to do well on assignments but also as a replaying of early relationships to authority, knowledge, and the world. "How should I write this essay?" is both a practical and imagined/unconsciously imbued question. On one hand there is the problem of completing an assignment and directions can be given to guide the student. On the other hand, the essay has to be written by the student, so there is no final answer to the question of how to write it. The idea of the countertransference helped me, and continues to help me, interpret and question my own reaction to students' engagements in my course. My own excitement, boredom, aggression, engagement, or disengagement reveals and carries my investments and histories of learning—both inside and outside of classrooms. What psychoanalytic theory has provided for me, along these lines, is a way to focus differently on the status of those kinds of questions and responses evoked by them. It allows me to focus on the ways that emotion and affect are always part of the learning environment.

Psychoanalysis makes education a problem because of the ways education demands a change in our orientation to the world. Psychoanalyst Adam Phillips (2004) writes that what we might need psychoanalysis in order

> to re-learn the nature of our satisfactions; the difference, say, between what we want and what we are supposed to want. You can teach people the facts of life, but you can't teach them sex. You can teach people about trauma, but you can't teach them their traumas. You can teach people about dreams, but you can't teach them to dream. You can teach people to listen, but you can't teach them what they will hear. (p. 798)

Phillips' point, for me, is that education cannot save us from the complications of the lives we lead. These are the terms of engagement that interest me in my inquiries in education research: the idea here is that education is both solution and problem. What happens in classrooms is overpopulated with meanings; some of which we can make sense of and some of which we cannot. But Phillips is also commenting on the ways in which education implicates what we already know. The meanings we make in the world are often revisions of meanings rather than brand new ideas without context or reference, what Britzman (2003b) formulates as an "after-education," an idea to which I return in the next chapter. The idea here is that significant learning is often, if not always, going to contain elements of earlier forms of knowing and knowledge. Learning will be a lesson itself in accommodating what we find in the world as it brushes against what we've found before.

Britzman (2006) explains the psychoanalytic project relating to education in terms of education's need of a theory to help understand the kinds of discomfort associated with being in classrooms and the demands that lie therein. Of course it is not just psychoanalysts who notice that classroom life can put (to state it mildly) odd expectations and rules into effect. Students are asked to sit quietly for extended periods of time, defer their pleasure, follow arbitrary directions, and most of all to "behave" (see Eisner, 1991; Jackson, 1968). But psychoanalysts read these oddities differently. Britzman (2006) explains how early psychoanalysts noticed that young patients could often not bear to go to school (p. 169). "In education," she writes, "little scenes of civilization and unhappiness were being played out" (p. 169). Psychoanalysts had doubts about education as a cure-all benefit for society because of the ways that these odd rules instantiated pulls and tugs on the psyche of the students. The concern is that classroom life is marked by conflict, not just between teacher and student, but also among and also within students, among and within teachers. These are familiar questions in a classroom: Am I doing this right? Is this good enough? May I have permission to go to the bathroom? May I speak at all (see also, Jackson 1968)? These questions indicate psychic struggle about the worth of our work, about controlling our instincts, about learning that our ideas are not always welcome. All of these struggles are rooted in early life encounters and are replayed in the classroom. It could be said, then, that psychoanalytic ideas are always and already "in" teacher education, but they are not generally thought of using those particular frames of reference.

Psychoanalytic theory, of course, holds no monopoly on the suggestion that learning is complicated and brings further complications. Scholars in social studies education, curriculum theory, and teacher education find that learning defies direct description and exists in spaces between other, similarly complicated, phenomena. We know, for example, that a teacher's education is a battle between students' fantasies of teaching and the will of the teacher educator—vis-à-vis our own fantasies (Britzman, 2006). There is no simple relationship between teaching the curriculum and what it is that the individuals learning it take away and inject with meaning as they live their lives. There are incredibly complicated spaces between (and within) all parties in the schooling process; the curriculum writer, administrator, teacher, parent, student (Bullough & Draper, 2004). These are inherent critical issues in the process of a subject learning to become a teacher (e.g., Segall, 2002). Complexity theory is used to frame the emergence and co-dependence of non-linear systems playing out in classrooms (Cochran-Smith *et al.*, 2014). In education research, where students are learning and teachers are teaching, there is general acknowledgment that there is always more going on.

Psychoanalytic theories bring a particular kind of complexity to thinking about social studies education. One primary and foundational assumption is that, despite wishes and fantasies that teaching and learning are directly related, a fantasy at play in "outcomes"-based measures that circulate so widely and that we can somehow know the results of our ("best") practices, that these wishes cannot be anything but a fantasy assigning certainty to radically uncertain processes. Further, as teacher educators, we have a great deal of knowledge that informs our practice, but we often do not know what comes of our efforts. This makes social studies and teacher education, like psychoanalysis, both "terminable and interminable" (Freud, 1937; Felman, 1982). This is to say that although there is an "end" to a history class and an "end" to social studies (when a student graduates from high school, for example), there is also, and simultaneously, a quality of a never-ending story of learning.

In this book I am not attempting to fashion solutions to problems of practice. Rather, I aim to call attention to what gets in the way when we try to teach lessons in the hopes that attending to the difficulties of learning will allow us to tolerate the uneven and unsettling terrain of our lives in and around classrooms. My approach is in keeping with what Taubman (2012) calls the emancipatory stance toward psychoanalysis in which there is no goal of a final cure or resolution to problems. Rather, it "works toward deepening and helping us understand and articulate our inner lives without promising the result" in advance (p. 6). "Such a project," Taubman continues, "never assumes it knows in advance what is best for the patient or student or what the

outcomes of its endeavors will be" (p. 7). This represents, to me, an invitation
to think about teaching and learning as co-constituted by the teachers and
the students, all of their subjectivities, their own histories of learning, and
unconscious desires brought with them. We cannot know what will occur in
advance of the lesson being taught. This brings lively complexity to the surface of the work done in classrooms.

Social studies education, when done well, will make other complications
of the world more evident to students. There will be more, rather than less,
ambiguity as students become more and more fluent with the realities of social
and political life. This book is an attempt to explore, theorize, and discuss
what it would mean to consider the ways in which difficult knowledge—a
concept deriving its theoretical force from psychoanalysis—can be applied to
and implicated within a social studies education that considers its project to
be that of learning to be with others in the world.

Chapter Overview

In the next chapter, chapter two, I elaborate on Britzman's term "difficult
knowledge" as it was first used and built upon in her work. I also explore how
others have deployed the term in various domains of educational thought.
Trauma, crisis, and vulnerability are three states of engagement that surface
implicitly and explicitly in issues of learning about the tumultuous social
world and therefore include discussions of how those states inform, or are in
conversation with, the various purposes of social studies education.

Chapter three takes the view of difficult knowledge to be that which poses
a challenge to the nascent views of the world teachers and learning bring to
pedagogy. Where difficult knowledge is in one sense an encounter with the
suffering of others, this chapter takes difficult knowledge as also that which
instantiates a difficulty on the part of the learner. Here, difficult knowledge
is less about historical trauma (though that can be part of the story of course)
and more about the kinds of things that knowledge does to us aside from pro-
viding us answers, comforts, or credentials. In short, knowledge can unsettle
us and can feel like our undoing. In order to explore what a psychoanalytic
vocabulary can do to help understand what occurs in the name of a social
studies education, I put it in conversation with what I think are our most
promising teaching methods: discussion, deliberation, and the centrality of
controversial issues.

Chapter four considers difficult knowledge in the context of social studies teachers' encounter with a documentary film about post-Katrina New Orleans. In it, a psychoanalytic research methodology is explored with qualitative interviews in which the circuits of difficult knowledge are traced in participants' reactions to the film.

Chapter five is an exploration of Toni Morrison's novel *Beloved* and its uses as a tool to think about difficult knowledge, pedagogy, social studies, and teacher education as being populated with issues of unknowability, estrangement, and the ways in which knowledge feels like a burden. I use excerpts from research interviews to demonstrate and explore the ways that aesthetic objects, like film in chapter four and literature in this one, offer ways for people to explore new relationships to knowledge.

Chapter six concludes this volume by centering issues of multiple perspectives and the role of questions in social studies education. Like the two chapters before it, a text is used as the provocation. In this chapter, it is a nonfiction book, Naomi Klein's *The Shock Doctrine*. I explore a recurring question that arose in relationship to readings of that book over the course of the several semesters I taught it: Why didn't I know this before? I use that question to highlight the ways that significant learning makes us question on our prior experiences, extends the pedagogical encounter, and multiplies perspectives. Questions make for more questions, and I conclude the chapter with an elaboration on the centrality of questions for both psychoanalysis and social studies education, paying particular attention to the ways in which we should remain suspicious of answers that pose as understandings. I have an abiding interest in the development and extension of ideas and express my certainty that the ideas in what follows are already under revision and hope that they will continue to be so indefinitely.

References

Alcorn, M. W. (2013). *Resistance to learning: Overcoming the desire-not-to-know in classroom teaching.* New York, NY: Palgrave Macmillan.

Boler, M. (2004). *Democratic dialogue in education: Troubling speech, disturbing silence.* New York, NY: Peter Lang

Britzman, D. P. (1998). *Lost subjects, contested objects: Toward a psychoanalytic inquiry of learning:* Albany, NY: SUNY Press.

Britzman, D. P. (2000). If the story cannot end: Deferred action, ambivalence, and difficult knowledge. In R.I. Simon, S. Rosenberg, & C. Eppert, *Between hope and despair: Pedagogy and the remembrance of historical trauma* (pp. 27–58) Lanham, MD: Rowman and Littlefield.

Britzman, D. P. (2000). Teacher education in the confusion of our times. *Journal of Teacher Education, 51*(3), 200–205.

Britzman, D. P. (2003a). *Practice makes practice: A critical study of learning to teach.* Albany, NY: SUNY Press.

Britzman, D. P. (2003b). *After-education: Anna Freud, Melanie Klein, and psychoanalytic histories of learning.* Albany, NY: SUNY Press.

Britzman, D. P. (2006). *Novel education: Psychoanalytic studies of learning and not learning.* New York, NY: Peter Lang.

Britzman, D. P. (2009). *The very thought of education: Psychoanalysis and the impossible professions:* Albany, NY: State University of New York Press.

Britzman, D. P. (2013). Between psychoanalysis and pedagogy: Scenes of rapprochement and alienation. *Curriculum Inquiry, 43*(1), 95–117.

Bullough, R. V., & Draper, R. J. (2004). Making sense of a failed triad mentors, university supervisors, and positioning theory. *Journal of Teacher Education, 55*(5), 407–420.

Cochran-Smith, M., Ell, F., Ludlow, L., Grudnoff, L., & Aitken, G. (2014). The challenge and promise of complexity theory for teacher education research. *Teachers College Record, 116*(5), 1–38.

Eisner, E. W. (2001). *The educational imagination: On the design and evaluation of school programs* (3 ed.). New York, NY: Pearson.

Farley, L. (2009). Radical hope: Or, the problem of uncertainty in history education. *Curriculum Inquiry, 39*(4), 537–554.

Felman, S. (1982). Psychoanalysis and education: Teaching terminable and interminable. *Yale French Studies* (63), 21–44.

Freud, S. (1937). Analysis terminable and interminable. *The standard edition of the complete psychological works of Sigmund Freud,* Volume 23 (pp. 209–253) Trans. J. Strachey. London: Hogarth Press.

Jackson, P. W. (1968). *Life in classrooms.* New York, NY: Holt, Rinehart, and Winston.

Lacan, J. (1998). *The four fundamental concepts of psychoanalysis: The seminar of Jacques Lacan: Book XI.* Trans. A. Sheridan. New York, NY: W.W. Norton & Company.

Lortie, D. C. (1975). *Schoolteacher: A sociological study.* Chicago: The University of Chicago Press.

National Council for the Social Studies (NCSS). (2013). *The college, career, and civic life (C3) framework for social studies state standards: Guidance for enhancing the rigor of k-12 civics, economics, geography, and history* (Silver Spring, MD: NCSS).

Phillips, A. (2004). Psychoanalysis as education. *Psychoanalytic Review, 91*(6), 779–799.

Pitt, A.J., & Britzman, D.P (2003). Speculations on qualities of difficult knowledge in teaching and learning: An experiment in psychoanalytic research. *Qualitative Studies in Education, 16*(6), 755–776.

Segall, A. (2002). *Disturbing practice: Reading teacher education as text.* New York, NY: Peter Lang.

Simon, R. I. (2005). *The touch of the past: Remembrance, learning, and ethics*. New York: Palgrave.

Simon, R. I. (2014). *A pedagogy of witnessing: Curatorial practice and the pursuit of social justice*. Albany: SUNY Press.

Tarc, A. M. (2011). Curriculum as difficult inheritance. *Journal of Curriculum and Pedagogy*, 8(1), 17–19.

Tarc, A. M. (2013). "I just have to tell you": Pedagogical encounters into the emotional terrain of learning. *Pedagogy, Culture & Society*, 21(3), 383–402.

Taubman, P. M. (2012). *Disavowed knowledge: Psychoanalysis, education, and teaching*. New York, NY: Routledge.

Werner, W. (2000). Reading authorship into texts. *Theory & Research in Social Education*, 28(2), 193–219.

Zembylas, M. (2014). Theorizing "difficult knowledge" in the aftermath of the "affective turn": Implications for curriculum and pedagogy in handling traumatic representations. *Curriculum Inquiry*, 44(3), 390–412.

· 2 ·

DIFFICULT KNOWLEDGE

Encounters with Social Trauma in Pedagogy

This books recognizes and inquires into the ways in which we make a relation with the social world. Such relations are fashioned through experiences in the world and interactions with various texts that represent it. Those experiences and interactions that invite or enliven our passionate responses, or prompt us to avoid them, are critical to understanding the ways in which individuals participate in (what we hope is and will continue to be) a democratic society. Those interactions and the cascading responses they provoke can be called difficult knowledge. To begin I offer two accounts of slavery from popular texts: one from a textbook and the other from an award-winning piece of narrative non-fiction.

> On the plantation, most slaves worked in the fields from sunup to sundown, six days a week. Although they were typically given Sundays off, many used that day to cultivate their own garden plots.
> Most slaves were periodically subject to physical abuse. Planters tended to use whips freely and sometimes even branded or maimed slaves to punish them. Many masters also sexually abused female slaves.
> The emotional torment imposed on the slave was as common as the physical abuse. ...
> Parents and children were frequently separated on the auction block. One way many slaves coped with these traumatic separations was by substituting "fictive kin" for blood ties. ...A great number of slaves also turned to the Christian religion for comfort. (Nash, 1994, p. 86)

The above excerpt is from a traditional American History textbook, *American Odyssey*. The text is describing the life of slaves in the antebellum South of the United States. Note the ways in which the facts of the slaves' lives are presented—hard work, physical, sexual, and emotional abuse. The paragraphs allude to physical and emotional pain and also the comfort of organized religion. This account is, I think, rather typical of textbook accounts of slavery in which abuse and hardship are represented, yet somehow distanced. To illustrate that distance, consider a second account of the life of slaves written by Ta-Nehisi Coates (2015) in his book *Between the World and Me*.

> *Enslavement was not merely the antiseptic borrowing of labor—it is not easy to get a human being to commit their body against its own elemental interest. And so enslavement must be casual wrath and random manglings, the gashing of heads and brains blown out over the river as the body seeks to escape. It must be rape so regular as to be industrial. There is no uplifting way to say this. I have no praise anthems, nor old Negro spirituals. ...The soul was the body that fed the tobacco, and the spirit was the blood that watered the cotton, and these created the first fruits of the American garden. and the fruits were secured through the bashing of children with stovewood, through hot iron peeling skin away like hulk from corn. It had to be blood. It had to be nail driven through tongue and ears pruned away. (p. 103)*

Both of these excerpts represent slavery. Both of these accounts take as fact the abuses of slavery. The first provides hints at comfort, though, by including phrases about days off and focusing on the coping rather than the tumultuousness of being enslaved. The second details the realities in ways that are more intimate. Both of these accounts take as fact the ways in which Christianity and slavery were related. Yet the second refuses its comforting narrative and gives over to the violence exacted on the bodies of the human beings who were made into slaves.

When students interact with the social studies, they are much more likely to encounter a text like the first one. It states facts but does not get too close to them. The second provides a more vivid representation and is likely to invite a much different encounter should a student be invited to read it. How do teachers and students choose to engage (or not) with a topic, like slavery, that codifies the worst parts of who we are to each other? Do we choose one path over the other? Do we choose the textbook version and, if we do, what are we avoiding? If we choose Coates's version, or use it to augment the curriculum, then what might occur? Might students become upset? Might they already know of the vivid trauma because it is their own family history? Might they not care? Might they laugh? What worries does the teacher have in instantiating such a lesson? What theories, concepts, modes of understanding are available to chart a course of action? Just as with any lesson, we cannot know the lesson in advance of its teaching. But what I think we do know is that inviting students to engage with a social world—present or historical—that is populated with violence, suffering, loss and devastation is inviting a host of complexities that can be called "difficult knowledge."

Defining Difficult Knowledge

Difficult knowledge locates a pedagogical relation within a particular situation that can arise from within the content (e.g., the Holocaust) or the context (e.g., a particular student's suffering). Difficult knowledge is a recognition of the unsteadiness of one's understanding of the world and our place in it that comes about through learning. In learning what we did not want to know, sometimes we lose our balance. Difficult knowledge is an orientation toward learning about the tumultuousness of society, recognizes the tumultuousness of our orientations to it, and further takes uncertainty as a central feature of the learning encounter. Difficult knowledge is a walk toward the ways in which that tumult can make one feel diminished, worried, guilty, sad or, alternatively, victorious, justified, and certain about a course of action.

The domain of inquiry that might be called difficult knowledge studies assumes a defended subject. The centrality of the defended subject to the relational situation of difficult knowledge suggests that the self is not ever quite aware of what the self needs, other than to be protected from discomfort. Discomforts, unique according to the individual, are common to the situation of difficult knowledge because of how things that fit in their places no longer have a place to go. This is to say our view of the world is shaken. If we had the privilege of not knowing that violence is systematically perpetuated in particular places onto particular bodies, we might work to defend ourselves from that knowledge. We might try to justify that violence. Or we might feel guilty about it. In any event, this difficult knowledge needs new places to go. New conceptual apparatus are called into being. The pedagogical relation of difficult knowledge can instantiate new ways of thinking in relationship to the world, and perhaps that is the most hopeful face of difficult knowledge studies. But those new ways of thinking may not be taken up in time to prevent the next trauma or to mitigate a current crisis. We just cannot know.

The first use of the term difficult knowledge is found in Britzman's (1998) essay "'That Lonely Discovery': Anne Frank, Anna Freud, and the Question of Pedagogy." The questions under consideration in that chapter have to do with the multi-directional timescales located in discussions of Anne Frank's diary as a pedagogical object. The diary is not just an artifact of a particular time and place. There are, rather, three temporal locations all operating simultaneously in relationship to the text: "the time of the writing, the time of finding and publishing the diary, and our own time of pedagogical engagement" (p. 114). Britzman identifies crucial aspects of learning at each of these temporal locations. First, at the time of the writing Anne Frank's diary represents a terrible learning and at the same time represents a learning about her own self, her coming of age, into sexual awareness, and within the confines of a genocidal regime. The diary is an account of the horrors of Nazi policy written by a girl who is also struggling with issues of adolescence. Second, at the time of the finding and publishing of the diary, there was a struggle over whether and which knowledge was appropriate for a readership. At this time there were debates and controversies (something to which social studies educators are attracted) about whether the diary should be represented as a story of Jewish persecution or of human perseverance and hope. And, finally, in the period of our pedagogical engagement we explore the complicated nature of reading about the suffering of another for the sake of our lesson plans in the present. Britzman's essay is a deliberation on the pedagogical situations that occur when confronted with the dilemmas of living and dying, vulnerability, hopefulness, and disappointment.

Within this context, readers are introduced to difficult knowledge via the following passage:

> In our own time, which, after all, is never just our own time, how can we grapple with the stakes of learning when the learning is made from attempts at identification with what can only be called difficult knowledge? The term of learning acknowledges that studying the experiences and the traumatic residuals of genocide, ethnic hatred, aggression, and forms of state-sanctioned—and hence legal—social violence requires educators to think carefully about their theories of learning and how the stuff of such difficult knowledge becomes pedagogical. This exploration needs to do more than confront the difficulties of learning from another's painful encounter with victimization, aggression, and the desire to live on one's own terms. It also must be willing to risk approaching the internal conflicts which the learner brings to learning. Internal conflicts may be coarsened, denied, and defended against the time when the learner cannot make sense of violence, aggression, or even the desire for what Melanie Klein calls the "making of reparation." (p. 117)

This first mention of difficult knowledge takes the form of a series of demands. The first demand difficult knowledge places on us is a requirement that educators think carefully about their theories of learning and what it is, exactly, that we are supposed to be learning from violence that is often legally sanctioned. There is a difficulty we can all recognize when making lesson plans out of the suffering of another. In this case, it is a recognizable difficulty to teach the lessons of the Holocaust because of its potential to introduce all sorts of emotions into the classroom and because emotions are, as we know, unruly things.

However, there is second demand that requires us to go beyond understanding an historical situation and move toward the ways in which learners bring a conflicted self to the scene of learning in the present. The idea of conflicted self is a foundational idea from psychoanalysis that acknowledges a part of ourselves that protects us from discomforts. This part of the initial offering of difficult knowledge makes a further demand, one that requires a focus on what learning from another's suffering does to and for us as we learn. Thinking carefully about our own theories of learning would have us make cautious interpretations about the stories we tell about the purposes of an education, and particularly about what lessons can be learned from devastation. There is the problem of the atrocity as well as the problem of the learner being able to tolerate learning from it.

Difficult knowledge is therefore an invitation to think about pedagogy from the vantage of the complications it introduces for learners and teachers in the attempt to learn from, rather than only learn about the world, where such a learning from requires another demand—"an interest in tolerating the ways meaning becomes…fractured, broken, and lost, exceeding the affirmations of rationality, consciousness, and consolation" (Britzman, 1998, p. 118). Difficult knowledge is, therefore, a focus on what gets in the way of learning a lesson from history.

Our Own Time Is Not Our Own

Social studies education is implicated in the idea of difficult knowledge from the very beginning of Britzman's (1998) definition. If our own time is never just our own time, we start our study of history, one of the four central disciplines of social studies, from the idea that we are in the middle of something ongoing and that this something is shared and therefore social. Difficult knowledge here is elaborated as "studying the experiences and the traumatic residuals" of history and historical content that is, as Freud writes, "essentially a series of murders of people" (*cf.* Britzman, 1998, p. 129). Britzman stages this introduction of difficult knowledge while undertaking an inquiry into the dynamic interplay between "being told too much and knowing too little" that occurs when one attempts to engage in learning about the unimaginable but terrifyingly real situations of genocide. Pedagogy is fragile from the very beginning because of the matching fragility of the structures in place for us to make sense of ourselves in the world.

As the psychoanalyst Adam Phillips (2014) explains, "Freud wants us to be wary of our temptation to make catchphrases out of history" (p. 7) and that, for Freud, "history is always more horrifying than we can let ourselves know" (p. 7). But why would this be? As pre-service social studies teachers begin their certification programs, one of the questions I pose early on is about the purpose of teaching and learning history. Many of the student first profess their "love" of the subject. Then, among the most common responses, and I doubt this will come as much to surprise to those within or beyond social studies education, is that we learn history so to avoid repeating its mistakes. What could be horrifying about this? For starters, it may be a little startling to think that the subject we "love" and our work in classrooms with it will be making lessons out of events from the past that were never meant to be part of lessons and that from this beginning we are walking on shaky ground. What is there to love about the Holocaust? We acknowledge that horrible things happen and then we are tempted to say that they occurred for a reason, or that they occurred but that the suffering was not in vain. Our time is not just our time because others have not only built the societies in which we live but also because those others are used as resources to make a life that is bearable. Difficult knowledge has something to do with the difficulties of (even thinking about) turning someone else's pain into a lesson plan so that some indeterminate and future other will not similarly suffer. If we acknowledge the horrors of history, then we acknowledge that horrible things happen and that these horrible things are sometimes the reasons why we are the particular "who" we are.

But perhaps we should not be allowed to be comforted by the narrative that we learn from our mistakes. This is an implication of the idea of difficult knowledge. However, thinking in alternative ways about the purposes of such inquiry requires a shift in thinking about the uses made of suffering and trage-dy in pedagogy. Ta-Nehisi Coates's (2015) work forcefully underscores such a point. In considering the ways in which racial violence persists into the 21st century, Coates is emphatic in his view that learning about the suffering and death of others not be allowed to provide comfort or to become a celebrated lesson plan. He writes:

> You must resist the common urge toward the comforting narrative of divine law, toward fairy tales that imply some irrepressible justice. The enslaved were not bricks in your road, and their lives were not chapters in your redemptive history. They were people turned to fuel for the American machine. Enslavement was not destined to end, and it is wrong to claim our present circumstance—no matter how improved— as the redemption for lives of people who never asked for the posthumous, untouchable glory of dying for their children. (p. 70)

Coates's (2015) writing, an address to his son but whose intended audience is largely white liberal America, points toward a disruption in the narrative that history is learned to avoid a repetition of mistakes. That progress narrative is problematic in Coates's view in that it reduces the particularity of human lives to a history lesson. It is a different vantage point on history to think that slavery was not destined to end. And even though it did end, that does not make the fact of slavery better, or redemptive, because "slavery is not an indefinable mass of flesh. It is a particular, specific enslaved woman, whose mind is as active as your own" (p. 69). Coates's view points toward a purpose of history that does not look toward a better future but is rather a view of the present which acknowledges "that no promise is unbreakable, least of all the promise of waking up at all" (p. 71). This locates the problem and promise of history education in the moments of lives that are being lived in the here-and-now. Without a narrative or hope of redemption, Coates's implication is a difficult one that may brush up against despair. However, a recognition of the universal truth that is our vulnerability to injury and, ultimately, death, is not necessarily hopelessness. For Coates, hope is located in the particularities of the ways people navigate, and struggle within (p. 71) their lives with a recognition rather than disavowal of that radical condition of precariousness.

Internal Conflicts the Learner Brings to Learning

However, Britzman's initial discussion of difficult knowledge acknowledges a need to go beyond the consideration of the difficulties of learning about another's painful encounter and to the "interior lives" of teachers and students. The kinds of conflicts that are elicited in the structure of difficult knowledge are present as the central concerns of psychoanalysis. Britzman (1998) articulates "the heart of psychoanalytic work is an ethical call to consider the complexity, conflicts, and play of psyche and history. These are the conflicts," she continues, "that education seems to place elsewhere" (p. 133). Britzman is clear about a pedagogical problem existing significantly in the fact of education's disavowal of our ambivalence toward knowledge. We are conflicted about knowing about the world because so often such learning means learning about loss. Sometimes learning means a certain loss itself. We might have to give up old stories and ways of knowing and that might feel like losing something. Making a relation to difficult knowledge means being able to recognize that there is knowledge that we simultaneously do and do not want to have. In particular, she writes that there is little hope to be found "where we ask students to engage with difficult knowledge of life and death without acknowledging the war within and without thinking about how pedagogical idealizations might coarsen the psyche's capacity to respond" (p. 133). History, therefore, is suggested as a location in which we find a tense knot between the past as represented in social science and the personal histories from which we make sense of who we are in relation to those narratives.

Psychoanalysts recognize an important aspect of history that critical historians also recognize; that the past has been narrativized into what we recognize as "history" and then utilized to support particular purposes. But as Phillips (2002) writes below, there is yet another crucial factor to the ways in which meaning is made in relation to these narratives.

> Whether it is in restaurants of galleries, or reading lists or history books, or television costume dramas, a past has been arranged for us…in which an individual or a group or an institution agrees to persuade us that this particular version and bit of the past should matter to us now. …It directs our attention and tries to fashion our sense of ourselves, and what these selves are supposed to want. But however seductive or persuasive or convincing this exhibition, this narrative, this costume drama is, its coercions are tempered by whatever else is going on inside ourselves at that time. (p. 145)

This "inside" is never really just our own self, but these social experiences are certainly experienced as an individual. There is no denying subjectivity. This subjective experience of the world is dependent upon history rendered in many different ways, among them is the formal history curriculum but not the least of the ways are our own personal histories (which, of course, have always existed within those official histories). Interiority, internal conflict, and the "war within" are each terms that psychoanalysis offers to aid in conceptualizing the subjective experience of learning and being. Here, learning is not just the ability to take in and then deploy knowledge on an achievement test. Instead, learning is considered as occurring in more substantial or profound instances where our views of the world and how it works are challenged. The conflict that is inherent in learning has to do with the psychoanalytic idea of "resistance to knowledge" (Britzman, 1998, p. 18). Britzman goes so far as to say that such "resistance is a precondition for learning" (p. 18).

Resistance in education generally denotes one of two things: a positive, politically oriented resistance to power as advocated by critical pedagogy, or an unwillingness for a student to perform according to the teacher's wishes. In psychoanalysis, though, resistance is couched somewhat differently. Felman (1982) conceptualizes resistance not in terms of the opposite of learning, but part and parcel to it. Pitt (1998) discusses resistance as the "resounding 'no' in the face of new and difficult knowledge" (p. 536). Resistance, in this view, ought to be thought of as part of an *engagement with* knowledge rather than outside of engagement (Garrett & Segall, 2013; Segall & Garrett, 2013).

What acknowledging defenses like resistance demonstrates is the idea that learning is always an ongoing work in progress fraught with a desire to have things be otherwise. We experience things prior to our understanding them, and our new understandings then shine new light on them and reframe those old events into new stories. This is what psychoanalysts call "deferral" or "afterwardsness" (Britzman, 2000a, p. 30). Something may remind us of a lesson or an experience, and in that moment the knowledge carries a new meaning. In a novel, a plot twist forces us to recast a prior understanding in light of new developments. In education, something to which to which we have been consciously opposed may return as a favored idea.

Thus, we can say that there is an inner battle being waged at all times between this knowing and forgetting, knowing and not wanting to know. Difficult knowledge is constitutive of this battle and vice versa. What Britzman (1998) is inviting in her invocation of this inner world is a consideration of social upheaval, war, violence, and suffering as challenging our views of the world, tempting us to both "know" and "forget" that we are capable of such atrocity and vulnerable to it. We are, it must be acknowledged, both vulnerable to and capable of atrocious behavior. Because of this, a social studies lesson about poverty or racism may be experienced as an accusation, and questions may be used as weapons: "Well, what are we supposed to do about this? Talking about it only makes it worse." These reactions potentially communicate discomfort with knowledge. They can signal, as Todd (2001) writes, an interaction that can produce affective feelings of guilt in students where the guilt "signals to the self, in the moment of articulation, that one is implicated in a wrong committed against another." Whether the guilt manifests itself as feelings of having not done enough to help, being undeservedly privileged, or being made to feel guilty unnecessarily, "Guilt carries with it the devastating idea that one has the potential to harm others without intention, and that this idea is itself too painful to bear" (p. 604). Although the guilt is personally experienced, it is in relation to a pedagogical scene in which something of the world is presented as a lesson. The outside meets the inside and blurs the boundaries between them. Difficult knowledge centers the features of such blurred boundaries and allows for a focus on the affective dimensions of pedagogy.

Difficult Knowledge in the Pedagogical Relationship

In an essay extending her discussion of difficult knowledge, Britzman (2000a) articulates the function of Anne Frank's diary as an object around which inquiries need to be made about the Holocaust but and also how and why particular objects function as objects of controversy. Just as there were debates about how the diary ought to be represented, there are debates about what should be taught in social studies (as I explore further in the next chapter). Controversy, when reduced to the style of a right/wrong or this/that, debate, functions as a defense against the encounter with difficult knowledge. In the pedagogical sense of difficult knowledge, the relation opens onto possibilities for new conceptual structures, including those that allow for implication of learners into their own learning.

Here, Britzman (2000a) brings difficult knowledge into focus as a way to acknowledge the possible uses of terrible and terrifying histories. The problem, of course, is that there is nothing anyone can do to bring back Anne Frank or to prevent the Holocaust or any other atrocity that has occurred. And it is not enough to say, again, that we learn history so that we do not repeat its mistakes. Rather, difficult knowledge is used as a term to acknowledge that mistakes constitute the human experience and that we are always in certain proximities to loss, violence, and injustice that are often not "mistakes" at all. They are the result of intentional and legal decisions. The Holocaust, just like slavery, was not a mistake, and this can be a horrifying realization. Not only was the Holocaust consciously enacted, it was done so with the very tools of modernity that were supposed to, and continue to be supposed to, provide everyone access to progress and the good life. So what can a lesson hope to accomplish? Britzman's (2000a) articulation of the pedagogical potential of encountering these notions revolves around attachments to the objects and texts attesting to it, which are such that students and teachers might:

> make from the diary new meanings in their own lives; to become attentive to pro-found suffering and social injustices in their own time; to begin to understand the structures that sustain aggression and hatred; and to consider how the very questions of vulnerability, despair, and profound loss must become central to our own concep-tualizations of who we each are, not just in terms of reading the diary as a text but also in allowing the diary to invoke the interest in the work of becoming an ethical subject. (p. 29)

Taken from the view of teaching, then, this quote provides social studies ed-ucators and researchers with some troubling prospects. How is it exactly, that we invite students to attend to "profound suffering"? What does it mean to center vulnerability, despair and loss as we work through our competing roles as teachers? What place do these questions have in social studies? We are taken into the notion that a study of the traumatic past must acknowledge that different, deferred, timeline from that of linear history and help students understand that there are processes and structures in place today that allow for and indeed promote suffering and injustice.

For example, in addition (or instead of) debating whether the US should have dropped atomic weapons on Japanese people in 1945, questions could be asked about the relations between human beings and how decisions are related to violence. Encounters could be invited about the ways humans were reduced to a cost, about the ramifications of the bombing since, and about the current dangers of nuclear devastation (which are in fact quite high). There is, of course, nothing inherently wrong with having students interpret the documents and question which arguments have the most merit. However, such an engagement does not allow students an engagement with the fact that history 1) cannot be changed, no matter who wins the "debate" and 2) that history persists into the present through nuclear proliferation, memorializa-tion, and questioning.

When Britzman (2000a) writes of the study of genocide, ethnic hatred, aggression, and forms of state-sanctioned and therefore legal social violence, she is writing about a great deal of the content under the purview of social studies curriculum and not just history. Forms of legal violence would include any study of war and conquest, which would by extension include things that might more conservatively be called "exploration." There is, in other words, no avoiding the dilemmas of difficult knowledge in the social studies curriculum, be it in geography, economics, civics, or history. Even if there is an absence of direct or explicit attention given over to the affective registers called in question, this view of the pedagogical relation acknowledges their presence. This view of teaching would not avoid debate or controversy, but it would acknowledge and be explicit about the ways that meanings will shift and change over time. This view of teaching would invite teachers and students into thinking about devastating histories in ways that do not predict or prescribe what will be done with that learning. Understanding of the social world follows the development of a conceptual apparatus built in response to the difficulties of understanding, and everything we do is about managing that suspended understanding.

In sum, the term difficult knowledge was initially used in the discussion of pedagogy in relationship to Anne Frank's diary, its reception, the disputes over its contents, and its implications for learning about society. But Britzman (2000a) further draws on the situation of difficult knowledge by implicating the massive social violence within the confines of teacher education. The list of twentieth century atrocities is alarming, from the Holocaust to the war on terror that greeted the twenty-first century. These are all present in the social studies curriculum, but a consideration of the processes that underwrite such horrors escapes disciplinary confines and implicates our work in other ways as well. Britzman writes that "all of these events should remind us of our present implication in world-making catastrophe" (p. 201). If teachers and teacher educators are part of the project of making the world a more just, more equitable, more safe, more tolerant place, then the implication is also that teacher educators are equally participating in the processes inherent in making the world the way it is. It is not only difficult to imagine horrific violence being exacted upon us, it is also horrific to imagine that we are participating, wittingly or not, in violence upon others. This again brings difficult knowledge of the past, the study of history, into the present as the location of significance.

What Britzman (2000a) is moving toward in such an argument is that the education of teachers ought to be considered in a much more expansive, much more elaborated way than the still significant, but too limited issues of "daily encounters of selves facing one another in a classroom" that highlights the "intimate problem of how one becomes affected by knowledge" (p. 201).

I will move to elaborate the ways in which this kind of view applies to social studies education in the next chapter, but for now I will continue to focus on understanding how historical violence and trauma function as a focal point.

Difficult Knowledge as Encounters with Representations

Britzman's collaboration with Alice Pitt (Pitt & Britzman, 2003) centers difficult knowledge as "a concept meant to signify both representations of social trauma in curriculum and the individual's encounters with them in pedagogy" (p. 755). This sense of difficult knowledge brings into focus the relation between a representation—a film, photograph, poem, narrative, painting, story, etc.—and an individual expected to do something with that representation. Difficult knowledge involves and implicates both the individual students and teachers as well as both the curriculum and pedagogy as they encounter together various media texts. The ability to produce such representations through the rapid proliferation of, and the democratization of access to, camera and film-making tools coincided with the twentieth century's list of violent and oppressive situations. It became much more likely that someone far away, "safe," from such situations could encounter a photograph depicting horrific scenes of brutality in the throes of apartheid in South Africa or in a postcard of a lynching in the South of the United States.

Twentieth-century technologies of representation have made it much easier to bring them into classroom contexts. Teachers can show their students images of lynching, starvation, mass murder, gun violence (in schools, too), and other kinds of suffering. Difficult knowledge, as a term, invites us to consider that there are likely to be a host of issues of which we are unaware that are brought to the fore when we encounter such images. Although teachers may be able to foster a pedagogical situation in which students use the violent past to situate themselves in relationship to a civics education that focuses on forward-thinking projects of fairness and kindness, they also may be tempted to use such representations in ways that are less helpful.

Perhaps this is why Britzman (2006) cautions against the teacher being too quick to capitalize on the ways that students are intrigued, indeed fascinated, by, representations of suffering. Teachers often carry a desire for students' interest. I know I do. It may be tempting, then, to use whatever teachers know will interest them, particularly in the context of schooling, in which student apathy and disengagement are such a common and widely reported phenomena. Within this context, having a group of students pretend that they are Anne Frank "hiding" under their desks or throwing paper balls across overturned desks to simulate trench warfare is understandable. Showing images and films that have a high production value like *Saving Private Ryan* or *Hotel Rwanda* can compel attention not only because of the historical and social issues but also because of the psychic invitations such films provide. There are reasons why those films seem to work so well to question, as Marcus (2005) suggests, issues of evidence, perspective, and empathy. Those are critical skills for students to practice. However, the construct of difficult knowledge invites us to recognize a host of other things operating at the level of emotion and affect. Crucially, these domains are seen as central to the project of understanding the social world and our experiences in it.

What I mean is that although there are certainly pedagogical opportunities in screening such films, it is uncommon that teachers or students consider the ways in which encountering those objects can remind us of our vulnerability and dependency on others to remain living. Difficult knowledge orients us toward paying attention to those risky thoughts. But also, there is a caution about the ways in which the teacher can take advantage of the psychic pulls of such encounters. Britzman (2006) writes:

> The urges to prevent what has already happened through the enactment of its violence, through shocking students into understanding, through forcing the others to undergo what the self cannot tolerate, indeed to punish the students with knowledge, all of these actions place the pedagogy in the [position of preventing students from making meaning of such a history] (p. 147).

This passage is written in relation to a teacher who has his students imagine being the victims of genocidal violence and calls into question such a strategy. I can imagine arguments being made about the worth and affordances of such a simulation, but the point here is that we are forced to ask the question about knowledge: Does such an intensely emotive or affective encounter come to have a meaning for students? If so, how? Or, how does such an encounter prevent or foreclose thinking altogether? These are the questions that Britzman's definitions have raised in relationship to difficult knowledge.

However, despite the troubles that are instantiated by difficult knowledge, the point here is not to avoid it further. Indeed, there are amazing possibilities in engaging with difficult knowledge, which is a further facet of its difficulty. Dori Laub (Felman & Laub, 1992) argues that the Holocaust is a microcosm of human experience and that our engagement with it brings us face to face with questions we often are able to ignore.

> The listener can no longer ignore the question of facing death; of facing time and its passage; of the meaning and purpose of living; of the limits of one's own omnipotence; of losing the ones that are close to us; the great question of our ultimate aloneness; our otherness from any other; our responsibility to and for our destiny; the question of loving and its limits; of parents and children; and so on. (p. 72)

Laub argues that the hope of this engagement is that students will talk about their affective attachments to the testimonies offered as texts, articulating what they find difficult, and in this speaking play with new meanings and new attachments to meanings. Although acknowledging the abhorrent nature of an historical trauma like the Holocaust, there is a simultaneous acknowledgment of the way this engagement can serve to cultivate an examination of the great existential questions of human life. In my experiences with secondary and post-secondary social studies students, there is often anger in these moments of encounter with difficult knowledge. This anger occurs not necessarily when discussing the Holocaust but when talking about contemporary examples of difficult knowledge such as structural inequality or institutional racism. When a student's sensibility about the world is disquieted, the disquieted individual seeks to steady themselves and their now-turbulent footing in the way they experience the world. This steadying is not always pleasant. Anger can be directed at the teacher and manifested as accusations of bias and ideological imposition. Students may lament the loss of human lives and become sad. Or they may be happy and comforted by the realization that it is "other people," who are suffering, but they are safe. There can be a profound confusion about what to do now. Some students, as described above, will feel guilt. If the goal of a social studies education is to promote the development of ethical subjectivities (i.e., the good citizen), it is imperative that we look not only at the ways in which sadness or guilt come into play when engaging difficult knowledge, but also at the ways in which students resist this kind of development and the manner in which teachers avoid fostering it.

Difficult Knowledge Studies

Difficult knowledge has gained footing in education research as a lens to understand the complex work of students' (and teachers' and researchers') engagement with these issues related to teaching and learning about historical trauma. Perhaps most significantly, Roger Simon's (2000, 2005, 2011, 2014) research centers similar issues and draws on the notion of difficult knowledge to help frame investigations as to the varied and murky processes involved in commemorative practices of histories of violence. Simon's inquiries into how various curatorial and pedagogical practices have come to have pedagogical impact help shape a field one might call "difficult knowledge studies."

Simon (2000) suggests that the issue in encountering the violent past "is not only what gets remembered, by whom, how, and when, but, as well, the problem of the very limits of representing and engaging events that in their extremity shock and resist articulation into already articulated discourse (p. 7). In other words, there is a fundamental problem in learning about mass social trauma because the inadequacies of language make these issues in and of themselves difficult for anyone to understand. Simon recognizes the consequences of seeing media images, photographs, film, or text that bear witness to such issues as slavery and the Holocaust as naturally instantiating an avalanche of affect—sadness, despair, confusion. But the problem, as Simon frames it, has a great deal to do with the ways that most common social studies education uses these kinds of texts with already established purposes. "On such terms," Simon writes, "traumatic memories of others become object lessons meant to illustrate some significant historical moment, social process, or change and to provoke a compassionate helpful response" (p. 18). The problem, as Simon notes, is that such lessons are meant (most often, anyway) to help students remember content, to understand history, and do not attend to what such remembering does to the learner.

What signals difficulty for Simon (2011), what constitutes the difficult encounter, is a situation in which the representation "confronts visitors with significant challenges to their …expectations and interpretive abilities" (p. 433). Such an elaboration underscores the ways in which difficult knowledge is a situation in which a challenging demand is placed on a viewer/learner to understand. Discomfort and unease are hallmarks of the relation between a curriculum and a student confronting difficult knowledge. Those confrontations can result in re-thinking, making new relations to old stories, or they might give rise to controversy, anxiety, sadness and other unpleasant emotions. Simon also acknowledges the ways in which learners/viewers of such representations may be traumatized themselves, shocked beyond their capacity to respond, in relation to particular kinds of images or installations. The past is unsettled in the present "when one comes face to face with the task of inheriting the troubling consequences of the otherness of knowledge" (Simon, 2011, p. 434). Such an unsettling marks not only something difficult, but also makes new thought possible without, of course, guaranteeing anything in advance.

Studies utilizing difficult knowledge as a framing concept tend to involve the use of aesthetic texts such as photographs, films, theatrical performances, and literature. Most use an aesthetic text and then deploy psychoanalytic vocabularies in order to theorize and elaborate on the terrain of the encounters people have around and with these texts. For example, Paula Salvio (2009) takes difficult knowledge outside of the classroom and into the darkroom. In her analysis of the war photographs of Lee Miller, she deploys the construct of difficult knowledge to represent the complexities associated, and invited, with photographs meant to portray messages from war. She couples the photograph with the psychoanalytic construct of symbolization, which is the process by which experience is given sociality through the use of language, though it is always representative of a compromise between what is felt and what is available to say with the spoken word. Salvio is troubled, like Britzman, by the temptations that teachers and students might face in their uses of representations of violence. She worries that "the narrative practices associated with documentary realism, while exciting for teachers and students on many levels, can unwittingly reduce what are often traumatic experiences to consoling narratives that fit neatly into the structure of normalizing and stigmatizing discourse" (p. 526). The use of difficult knowledge is a theoretical lever that allows the movement from these troubling narratives of consolation toward a consideration of these images as ways to "challenge understandings of nationhood, citizenship, and norms of social belonging" (p. 526). This points out again the tension between, and attention to, the broader world of events outside and the affective torrents occurring inside.

Lisa Farley (2009) elaborates those conflicts in her consideration of history education as a site for conflict rather than its resolution. She utilizes the psychoanalyst Donald Winnicott's concept of disillusionment in order to frame the notion that learning from history is best conceptualized as developing a way to tolerate "the disillusionment of encountering the otherness that history both references and provokes on the inside" (p. 538). Disillusionment is a necessary experience in order for a child to grow into and tolerate the ambiguities of the social world. Such a stance evokes and extends Britzman's theory of difficult knowledge in that there is significant tangling between the "inside" of the learner and the "outside" that is society or historical narrative.

Many other scholars have engaged difficult knowledge from the vantage of museum studies and curation. Brenda Trofanenko (2011, 2014) identifies the ways in which curatorial practices have shifted to accommodate emerging views of learning that address the affective and emotional engagements with knowledge about war. Lehrer, Milton, and Patterson (2011) work from the location of public museums but, of course, frame their inquiry on the ways in which otherwise marginal discourses are brought into public view. They acknowledge the ways that encounter does not match with prevention, that narratives of "never again" are disappointing and empty, and that memory work is crucial but mysterious. Sara Matthews's (2013) work from inside museums engages the psychoanalytic practice of free association as method and presents in research an imaginary exhibit as an object open to interpretation. Such a practice begins from the point in the relation of difficult knowledge where the encounter leaves one unable to understand in the face of the facts that cannot be accommodated. Matthews exemplifies the ways in which such a state can be thought of as productive in that it "symbolizes the tension of feeling undone without reaching too soon toward representation" (p. 275).

But what would be wrong with such a move toward representation? What difficult knowledge studies seem to be teaching us in social studies is that sometimes the best lesson we can offer is that settled stories, comforting narratives, and certainty are rather dangerous. It seems to be the case that moving too quickly to answer the question of what can be made from histories of violence and loss puts us in jeopardy of foreclosing thought. Wodke (2015) draws on difficult knowledge and echoes Britzman's warnings about the comforts embedded in provisions of hopeful and redemptive narratives working to close down thought. This is in keeping with Elizabeth Ellsworth's (2005) notion of refusing narrative closure in that it acknowledges what difficult knowledge highlights—notably, that histories of loss and suffering are not closed and finished stories.

In too many instances, of course, the violence and suffering come not from the past but from conflicts occurring in the present. Zembylas's (2014, 2015) work utilizes and extends difficult knowledge by using poststructural and affect theories to theorize and forward a sense of education in conflict zones. Rather than having the relative privilege of witnessing conflict as a new idea in classroom spaces, Zembylas's studies occur in conflicted societies in which there is actually a rather pressing need for action. Although the idea that allowing stories to remain open and supporting learners' experiences with ambiguous or conflicting affective response is productive, there is also a need for critical action to occur. For Zembylas (2014), difficult knowledge requires an additional component that points toward the kinds of critique, activism, or strategic pedagogies that can allow for the kinds of living on in the midst of conflict and violence.

Difficult knowledge studies provide social studies educators and researchers a language for an engagement with the complexities inherent in aiding students' learning about the ways that societies underwrite, perpetuate, and sustain violence and injustice. The concept is central to the domain and project of social studies education, an idea which I return to in the next chapter. For now, though, I turn to the ways in which scholars from outside of education have concurrently been concerned with the same issues that difficult knowledge has raised. Indeed, the notion of difficult knowledge coincides with and reveals several preoccupations of the theorists and cultural critics who are making sense of contemporary life.

Contextualizing Difficult Knowledge: Trauma, Crisis, and Vulnerability

How to respond to the massive sites and processes of devastation is a question that is taken up in various ways by the humanities and cultural critics. Britzman's term, difficult knowledge, capitalizes on psychoanalytic insights about the circuits of learning, the unpredictability of pedagogy, and the ways in which classroom lives are tangled up with personal and social histories. It is a term that has most commonly aided other scholars in attending to the ways in which the traumas of others are represented as some sort of learning opportunity. These issues are part of a larger context of current social thought in which issues of politics and relationality are being deliberated. High-profile scholarship emerges in the settings of political philosophy and cultural criticism from authors such as Susan Sontag and Judith Butler. The field of "dark tourism' studies (Lennon & Foley, 2000) has grown in volume and considers the political and ethical grounds upon which travelers visit sites of unthinkable horrors, such as Auschwitz. In social studies education, however, there has not been a similar move. And let me explain why this is important. Social education is supposed to be the location for the cultivation of a sense of place in the world among others withvwhom we share concern and responsibility. There are people, social critics and philosophers among them, whose preoccupation is similar and often the same. As new patterns and trends emerge in society they precipitate new analyses of our relations to the institutions and structures out of which we make our lives; those analyses make patterns too. Out of those patterns, ideas crystalize such as that Britzman called "difficult knowledge."

In order to contextualize difficult knowledge within those currents and further elaborate its relation to social studies education, I will use three terms: trauma, crisis, and vulnerability. These three concepts are terms that social theorists have used in their analyses and, thus, are part of broader social discourses out of which difficult knowledge emerges. In many ways, each of these ideas have their roots in trauma theory, so I begin with trauma as a domain of inquiry. Difficult knowledge can identify a relation between the trauma of an historical event and the potential for trauma "in the very capacity to know" (Pitt & Britzman, 2003, p. 756). The next sustaining feature of difficult knowledge is the idea of vulnerability. In one sense there is difficult knowledge suspended in the recognition of the fact of our vulnerability to each other, to injury and to death. Another register vulnerability takes in relationship to difficult knowledge is in the ways in which vulnerability circulates within the moments of classroom encounters. The third plane of difficult knowledge has to do with the status of crisis. Here, I consider crisis by borrowing Berlant's (2011) term "crisis ordinariness" as a way to frame the current genre of understanding socio-political events. Adding to that, though, is the relationship between crisis and pedagogy that has been articulated by Felman and Laub (1992), Ellsworth (2005), Britzman (2009), and others. I present these three vantages from which to view difficult knowledge and then discuss their relationship to a social studies education that is open to the uncertainties and uneven terrain of teaching and learning about the social world.

Trauma

Trauma itself is a psychoanalytically inflected term that denotes the functioning of an event to effectively unsettle one's capacity to go on as before, and as such deserves initial attention before turning specifically to difficult knowledge. In the 1980s and 1990s a field of inquiry now referenced as "Trauma Studies" was taking hold in the academy. Cathy Caruth, Shoshana Felman, and others centered questions of living in the time after a traumatic event to understand that life is a negotiated relationship between psychical defenses and the desires to live. Trauma, Caruth (1996) writes, is not locatable in the simple or violent original event in an individual's past, but rather the way that its very unassimilated nature—the way it was precisely not known in the first instance—returns to haunt the survivor later on. (p. 4)

What Caruth points to is the fact that the trauma is not over when its instantiating event ends. It comes back, pulling the rug out from underneath the surviving individual who, after the event, has not been able to incorporate its consequences into their psychical apparatus.

Part of the reason this is so is because thinking about trauma is a way to understand a dimension of social living that involves death and survival and the oscillations between those two. What is traumatic is not the death of an individual. The death is often tragic, of course. But trauma is a relation to death that has to do with the kinds of living on that occur in the present and in relation to that event in the past. Therefore, what is traumatic is not the event, but the simultaneous "necessity and impossibility of responding to another's suffering or death" (Caruth, 1995, p. 101). When attempting to make some kind of lesson plan out of the Holocaust, lynching, famine, disease, or other social atrocities, the idea of trauma is not located in the past. The trauma is located in the relation to the past and acknowledges that there is simultaneously a need to rectify but it is impossible to address it. This is the complicated and multi-directional timeline of trauma.

Many of the features of difficult knowledge grow out of or bear strong relation to the assumptions growing out of trauma theory. Three key ideas that Caruth set into motion and around which trauma studies revolves, according Sara Matthews (2013) are

1) the notion that trauma is not an 'event' per se (e.g., a circumstance in which one sustains severe physical and/or psychic injuries), but rather the inability to fully experience or assimilate an event due to its overwhelming nature, a force which then continues to visit the survivor belatedly via a host of unmediated symptoms; 2) that the act of narration, within the particular conditions produced by the dynamics of testimony and witnessing, allows for the creative symbolization of experience and therefore holds recuperative potential; 3) that certain aesthetic objects, because of their ineffable qualities, are uniquely suited to trauma's symbolization. (p. 3)

What trauma theory provides, then, is a "powerful hermeneutic for linking events of extreme violence, structures of subjective and collective experience, and discursive and aesthetic forms" (Rothberg, 2013, p. xiv). What this means is that there is a link between the fact of the atrocity, the experience of it, and then how it comes to be enacted, represented, or worked through within the confines of written word, personal experience, or artistic practice. Such working through is a necessary component of finding some return to a world view that can contain the experience of trauma. Trauma's psychoanalytic rendering has to do with the effects and repeated unconscious enactments of a particular event around which those repetitions ripple.

The implications for social studies education of trauma theory lie in the connections between the content often pertaining to traumatic events (what other social studies scholars have called 'difficult histories') and the individual's encounter with this content. The difference between a pedagogy or stance toward social studies that is informed by trauma theory, psychoanalysis, and difficult knowledge is that these will always implicate the viewer, learning, and pedagogue into the dynamics of the traumatic event. This is to say that there is no "outside" to this dynamic, and likewise that there we cannot dispassionately consider an historical atrocity without at least brushing up against the affective registering of that experience. This is not to say that the viewer or learner or teacher is experiencing "the trauma" him- or herself. And it is not a guarantee or a recipe that would be able to predict the kinds of responses people will have in relationship to a particular representation. There is, though, the possibility of being involved in a dynamic kind of relationship with that traumatic event and its human toll that is explained in discussions of trauma theory.

Notions of trauma such as those described above have served to frame a wide body of literature addressing cultural issues and institutions, notably in the arts and museums. However, critiques of trauma theory have also begun to arise in ways that challenge the notion of difficult knowledge. One of the ways in which trauma theory is being critiqued occurs in light of the current social situation in which we find ourselves. Right now, the traumatic potential that presses upon us does not just come from history. Trauma, some posit, also comes from the present and the future in predictable ways. Notably, the "status of labor under globalization and the impact of climate change" provide sites of trauma that are unbound by (but, of course, not unrelated to) history (Rothberg, 2013, p. xiv). What this means is that there is a facet of social theories of trauma that asks us to unlink trauma from a past event. Now, trauma theorists are trying to account for the ways in which individuals and groups are dealing with the psychic costs of living with, and in relation to, events that we know will happen as a result of collective human activity.

For example, some utterly predictable catastrophes await us. One category of those will be fueled by climate change and will be recognized through mass migrations and responses to changing weather patterns. Another future catastrophe is something like a nuclear explosion, an event which has a chance of occurrence in any ten-year period somewhere between .001% and 7% (Global Challenges Foundation, 2016). Given that both of these instances are inextricably linked to political decision making, these are crucial dimensions for social studies education to consider and discuss. In thinking about citizenship education in relation to these developing ideas, it is worth acknowledging the trauma takes place "on the site of—and thoroughly embedded within—a system of violence that is neither sudden nor accidental" (Rothberg, 2013, p. xiv).

On one hand, Caruth (1995) provided a groundwork for trauma theories to be taken up into educational theory. Britzman's introduction of "difficult knowledge" is an example of that registering of trauma into the lexicon of education and teacher education. On the other hand, though, the way in which trauma theory implicates a focus on the past and its implications for the present is brought to its limit as current theorists have begun to shift their focus to the present and future. The ideas of vulnerability and crisis help to orient us toward that focus.

Vulnerability

Traumatic histories, presents, and futures all circulate in social studies education. Trauma studies serves to orient an understanding of the terrain in which events occur that cannot be accommodated by those who experience them. There are some things that move beyond our capacity for understanding. With this in mind as well as the unpredictable circuits of trauma, Britzman (1998) acknowledges that "the pedagogical staging of experiences of social violence must attend carefully to what the study of aggression might open" (p. 119). This is yet another demand for pedagogy in the situation of difficult knowledge.

One of those "whats" that may be opened upon the study of aggression is vulnerability. Vulnerability, the second relational term that aids in consideration of difficult knowledge, is related to trauma in that we are all subject to it. The universal condition of vulnerability is laid bare in situations of difficult knowledge. Judith Butler's (2004, 2010) elaboration of vulnerability can inform and elaborate on the careful caring for which Britzman calls. As Zembylas (2014) writes, Butler's work "allows for the emergence of fruitful openings that enable us to consider 'difficult knowledge' from an action-oriented perspective, without disavowing the psychical problematics embedded in this effort" (p. 400). Indeed, Butler attends to the psychoanalytic modes of relationality in her analysis that clearly draws from other theoretical perspectives including poststructuralism and feminism. The idea of vulnerability rests on the fact of our dependence on others to be alive. Butler (2010) writes of

> the irrefutable ways in which we are all subject to one another, vulnerable to destruction by the other, and in need of protection through multilateral and global agreements based on the recognition of a shared precariousness. (p. 43)

Such an acknowledgement presses upon social studies educators' tendencies toward civics education. Rather than putting the conversation in terms of compromise, justice, or the common good, Butler frames this as an issue of recognition, in this case of a shared precariousness. In this view, a recognition of our shared vulnerability and precariousness is a political project. Her work, just like Britzman's with difficult knowledge, is commenting upon encounters with the suffering of others. Both authors question how that encounter can lead to something other than a comforting narrative of redemption or palliation. Just as Britzman (2000a) suggests that learning from difficult knowledge means learning about the systems that sustain violence and aggression in our time, Butler's (2004, 2010) recent work has provided an in-depth discussion of how people come to encounter and understand such current manifestations. In Butler's case, the terms of engagement are with the photographs and documentary news footage coming out of war zones produced as part of the War on Terror. Butler takes vulnerability, something we might commonly understand as quite disconnected from social studies and demonstrates its clear political and social dimensions.

For Butler, vulnerability is a political idea. She deploys the idea in order to draw focus to the ways in which we devalue the lives of other people for our own convenient though illusory stories of safety and security. Butler (2004) identifies vulnerability as a persistent trait of our lives, writing that

> we all live with this particular vulnerability, a vulnerability to the other that is part of bodily life, a vulnerability to a sudden address from elsewhere that we cannot preempt. This vulnerability, however, becomes highly exacerbated under certain social and political conditions, especially those in which violence is a way of life and the means to secure self-defense are limited. (p. 29)

Butler simultaneously identifies the fundamental condition that we are always at risk of being injured as well as the fundamental recognition that people share uneven risks of injury. Further, she suggests that our lives are identified as intertwined with others' lives and that particular political and social situations make some more vulnerable than others. That is, vulnerability is not equitably distributed across nation-states, economic classes, race, gender, and sexual identifications. Such inequities play out all the time, of course, but become acute in times of war. For example, the citizens of Iraq are much more vulnerable than I am as a relatively well-off white male in the United States. Of course I am still at risk of injury because we are never fully protected or safe from harm. However, our vulnerabilities are related to our situations within fabrics of power. And it isn't until we are confronted with shocking images from war zones that we are able to rethink or reframe the politics that lead to such suffering. There is something necessary about some kinds of what Roger Simon (2011) calls a "shock to thought" in order to cause a sufficient disruption in people's interpretive frameworks. It is as though if we are not already attuned to injustice, then we need to be shaken in our encounters with and learnings about the world.

Butler's (2010) writing takes the reader closer into the processes at play when someone encounters a provocative image signaling trauma, loss, and/or death. The situation of difficult knowledge is one where the encounter with another's suffering can prompt a return to our own unconscious memories of being vulnerable to, and utterly dependent upon, others for our survival. Put most simply, in this view, our selves are always social, making it so that we are never quite belonging solely to ourselves. This view is in line with psychoanalytic views of identity that acknowledge the way we interpret society's rules shapes the way we route our desires into civil society (Freud, 1968). And it is also similar to psychoanalytic ideas of who we are because we are radically dependent on those who care for us for our first social studies lessons. In other words, this "means that we are vulnerable to those we are too young to know and to judge and, hence, vulnerable to violence; but also vulnerable to another range of touch, a range that includes the eradication of our being on one end and the physical support for our lives on the other" (Butler, 2010, p. 31).

The encounter with representations of catastrophe has the potential to instantiate an anxiety about our own vulnerability. There are several striking examples, from Kevin Carter's Pulitzer Prize winning photograph of a vulture in proximity to an emaciated Sudanese child to the photograph of a dead

Syrian boy, drowned in attempt to flee conflict, washed ashore. When we see a newspaper photograph of a child lying injured or dead, we may be shocked and our thoughts may turn to our own children, our own childhood, just as easily as we attend to the news contextualizing the image. We are invited to a thought where we acknowledge that not only are we vulnerable to injury, but of course the others with whom we share the world are vulnerable as well. Butler (2010) puts it thusly:

> the apprehension of the precarity of others—their exposure to violence, their socially induced transience or dispensability—is, by implication, an apprehension of the precarity of any and all living beings, implying a principle of equal vulnerability that governs all living beings. (p. xvi)

What Butler implies for the work of pedagogy is that being exposed to the suffering of other people will invoke the sense that the viewer is also at risk of suffering as well. Further, she is implying that a war photograph is not only identifying a personal story of suffering, it also indicates this "socially induced dispensability." The photograph of the dead child is not only evocative of sadness and empathy, it is evidence of a particular policy that exposed particular persons to violence and led to their death.

What encountering such an image can do, potentially, is collapse the distance between who we recognize as worthy of life and who we do not. Butler's (2004) term for understanding this distinction is "grievability," an idea that denotes that although some lives are grieved upon loss, others are not. We grieve the loss of an American soldier, but not the loss of the Iraqi boy. Being rendered "ungrievable" by widely circulating narratives paves the way for the kinds of policies that are enacted by the state. However, the shock of the photograph may allow for a pedagogical moment of suspension in those coordinates. Butler writes that such an encounter

> calls upon and enacts certain interpretive frames; [it] can also call into question the taken-for-granted character of those frames, and in that way provide the affective conditions for social critique. (p. 34)

What this means for social studies educators is that the provision of such disturbing images may be a potential way to open up the space for new ways of relating to old processes; it may instantiate a process whereby a thinker is pushed to the limits of their capacity to interpret and articulate an explanation. So it is that just as Pitt and Britzman's (2003) definition of difficult knowledge focuses on the encounters with representations of social and historical trauma,

Butler illuminates the functioning of photography and filmed footage from news media as powerful frames of vulnerability and precariousness.

This becomes an issue for pedagogy because of the ways people are taught not to have such a recognition. Butler's argument is that we misrecognize others' lives as not lives at all. Rather, we recognize some others as "terrorists" or "sympathisers" or "collateral damage." Recognition of vulnerability is a pedagogical project because of the ways that encountering the violence perpetuated against some others represented in photographs or documented in film can shift the frameworks of our understanding. In social studies education, such a calling into question of the taken for granted may be the best pedagogical outcome we can imagine and further underscores Britzman's (1998) stated need that we "explore how the learner comes to identify and dis-identify with difficult knowledge" (p. 119). Part of the work of a pedagogy informed by difficult knowledge in social studies education is identifying frames of, and obstacles to, recognition.

Vulnerability is a term that, again, is a social construct that can orient pedagogical lines of questioning. What living in the twenty-first century has come to mean is that "we each have the power to destroy and be destroyed, and that we are bound to one another in their power and this precariousness" (Butler, 2010, p. 43). Further, our emotional responses are "conditioned by how we interpret the world around us" (Butler, 2010, p. 34). This means that our most personally felt reactions can be used as materials for questions. Why do we feel a particular outrage for one person's suffering but not another's? What do these feelings indicate about our political commitments? What do they reveal about our aggression? How have our senses been attuned to particular lives lost and do we agree with that or not?

Vulnerability, the idea that we are beholden to one another, contributes to my idea of social studies education being the project of learning to be with others in the world. It recognizes that "who I am is nothing without your life, and life itself has to be rethought as this complex, passionate, antagonistic, and necessary set of relations to others" (Butler, 2010, p. 4). Such a complicated view of learning about the world and how others live and die within it presses upon our capacities of understanding. It is dependent upon a view of learning that holds that learning will occur through moments when understanding is a struggle. Sometimes that struggle can be related to crisis.

Crisis

Crisis has been considered as inextricably bound up with the terrain of learning and is intimately related to the ideas of vulnerability and trauma. Felman's (1992) provocative claim about teaching in any significant sense serves as a worthy beginning

> Teaching as such, takes place precisely only through a crisis: if teaching does not hit upon some sort of crisis, if it does not encounter either the vulnerability or the explosiveness of a (explicit or implicit) critical and unpredictable dimension, it has perhaps not truly been taught: it has perhaps passed on some facts, passed on some information and some documents, with which the students or the audience—the recipients—can for instance do what people during the occurrence of the Holocaust precisely did with information that kept coming forth but that no one could recognize, and that one could therefore truly learn, read or put to use. (p. 53)

Felman recognizes that for learning anything significant, anything worth learning about, crisis will be a feature. Britzman's (1998) inaugural use of difficult knowledge leaned on Felman's work regarding the ways in which bearing witness to trauma exacted a toll on the psyche. In this view the big external crisis meets the ordinary internal crisis that is learning. If crisis figures prominently in any learning worth its name, and if difficult knowledge is made from crises arising through systemic violence, then what it signifies is worth exploring. Here, I draw from Lauren Berlant's (2011) work, where she explores and elaborates on the ways that current social occurrences are largely organized around and oriented by crisis.

First, Berlant (2011) decouples crisis from trauma, positing that trauma is but one "genre" of dealing with a destabilizing event. Not everything that is crisis will be experienced as, or result in, a trauma. Second, and equally provocative I think, is that she discusses crisis in terms of an ongoing persistent feature of twenty-first century life rather than a unique event. Crisis, after all, is amplified through the 24-hour news cycle, social media, and profit-driven news media. Crisis is not an outlying event that flashes onto the scene. Furthering her elaboration of crisis and its ordinariness she writes that "the extraordinary always turns out to be an amplification of something in the works, a labile boundary at best, not a slammed-door departure" (p. 7) Crisis, therefore, is a genre of

> heightening interpretation…rhetorically turning an ongoing condition into an intensified situation in which extensive threats to survival are said to dominate the

reproduction of life. ...The genre of crisis can distort something structural and ongoing within ordinariness into something that seems shocking and exceptional. (p. 7)

Berlant points toward a conception of crisis that illuminates its grounding in processes and procedures that are ongoing. Read in this way, but always in reverse, the crisis can be a scene of learning. The crisis occurs when that taken-for-grantedness is foreclosed, it is less of an event than an affective structure of experience. Just as the trauma is not located in the event but what is left in its wake, crisis is the extended moment of not knowing what to do.

Perhaps what makes this pedagogical is that in such moments of experience we have to make our way somehow. In this making our way we are invited into new modes of relation with ourselves and with others; we are required to re-conceptualize and re-articulate the sense we make of the world. Berlant illustrates how such moments demarcate potential even as they press upon a requirement to improvise.

Social studies education is largely concerned with the crises that are codified in the official curriculum, but they are not typically rendered as such. The crises of the past that occurred in and through the upheaval of revolutions and the suffering of the planter's whip are told as largely sanitized narratives. However, the people occupying the classrooms in which we teach do experience crisis. In fact, Berlant (2011) sees our current social situation as one she calls "crisis ordinariness" (p. 10). Consider that students who are of high school age have grown up during ongoing war, consistent occurrences of mass shootings, economic collapse, and are faced with diminishing prospects of financial gain as well as climatic catastrophe: crisis ordinariness is the idea that crisis is the structuring category of our current time.

But crisis ordinariness is also a different way of thinking about the ways in which people live through devastation. Although it is true that particular conditions can produce a traumatic result, it is also true that people continue to live as they test out new ways to be in the world with no guaranteed result. Berlant's (2011) claim is that there are unprecedented conditions of social life to which our narratives and explanations have not caught up. Ubiquitous surveillance presses upon the notion of a citizen; global capital flows, climate change, and the like are taking us into uncharted waters, yet we still tend to cling to the narratives provided by meritocracy, freedom, democracy, and upward mobility. Berlant is making these observations not based on the academic literature but on the ways that people seem to live in the world; for example, the ways that people cling to stories of the good life and economic mobility. In so doing, she provides an attractive filter through which to see the work of social studies education.

The crisis here marks the slippage, the disjuncture between the things we think we believe in and that which is actually available to us. Difficult knowledge orients us toward the ways in which learning can, and often does, instantiate the crisis, and Berlant's rendering of crisis aids in identifying the structure of what can occur as a result, namely, that our stories can shift. Sometimes for the worst, but one hopes for the better.

Conclusion

Crisis, vulnerability, and trauma run through and constitute the conceptual apparatus of difficult knowledge. The socio-political understandings and orientations we have are co-constitutive of personally rendered ways of knowing and the encounter with representations of the "world out there." Difficult knowledge may invite us to think about the ways in which living in the world exposes our vulnerability to each other and how that vulnerability is a political, civic, historical, economic and geographic issue. It may help us think about how the traumas of the past and present defy our wishes for steady lessons to teach and learn. And it may beckon us toward thinking about a pedagogy that considers crisis as something of a potential for new thoughts in relation to old ideas.

And here we meet the fundamental challenge of difficult knowledge and its implications for teaching social studies. If we know that the representation of social trauma, suffering, or violence can instantiate enlivened reactions and make way for people to reconsider ideas, then can we make a lesson plan that capitalizes on this? Can we strategically use the lynching photograph? If so, what strategy can accommodate the conflicts of political violence as well as the conflicts that are inherent in learning?

Social studies education does, of course, engage conflict as part of what I think are its signature pedagogies: deliberation, discussion, and debate of controversial issues. Our "best" pedagogies ask students to take positions on an issue, make hypotheses about answers to questions, gather evidence, and make arguments. These are powerful strategies that are shown to engage learners in meaningful instruction. Yet they also only see the conflict as external. Britzman's (1998, 2009) insistence on the interiority of learning is perhaps the most crucial assertion that psychoanalysis can bring to social studies: that conflict exists as part of the learning encounter as much as it does in the competing accounts of the social issue under investigation.

References

Berlant, L. G. (2011). *Cruel optimism*. Durham, NC: Duke University Press.

Britzman, D. P. (1998). "That lonely discovery": Anne Frank, Anna Freud, and the question of pedagogy. *Lost subjects, contested objects: Toward a psychoanalytic inquiry of learning*. Albany, NY: SUNY Press.

Britzman, D. P. (2000a). Teacher education in the confusion of our times. *Journal of Teacher Education, 51*(3), 200–205.

Britzman, D. P. (2000b). If the story cannot end: Deferred action, ambivalence, and difficult knowledge. In R. I. Simon, C. Eppert, & S. Rosenberg (Eds.), *Between hope and despair: Pedagogy and the remembrance of historical trauma* (pp. 27–58). Lanham, MD: Rowman & Littlefield.

Britzman, D. P. (2006). *Novel education: Psychoanalytic studies of learning and not learning*. New York, NY: Peter Lang.

Britzman, D. P. (2009). *The very thought of education: Psychoanalysis and the impossible professions*. Albany, NY: SUNY Press.

Butler, J. (2004). *Precarious life: The powers of mourning and violence*: Brooklyn, NY: Verso.

Butler, J. P. (2010). *Frames of war: When is life grievable?* Brooklyn, NY: Verso.

Caruth, C. (1995). *Trauma: Explorations in memory*. Baltimore, MD: Johns Hopkins University Press.

Coates, T.-N. (2015). *Between the world and me*. New York, NY: Spiegel & Grau.

Ellsworth, E. (2005). *Places of learning: Media, architecture, pedagogy*. New York, NY: Routledge.

Farley, L. (2009). Radical hope: Or, the problem of uncertainty in history education. *Curriculum Inquiry, 39*(4), 537–554.

Felman, S. (1982). Psychoanalysis and education: Teaching terminable and interminable. *Yale French Studies* (63), 21–44.

Felman, S., & Laub, D. (1992). *Testimony: Crises of witnessing in literature, psychoanalysis, and history*. New York, NY: Taylor & Francis.

Freud, S. (1968). *Civilization and its discontents* (J. Strachey, Trans.). New York, NY: W.W. Norton.

Garrett, H. J., & Segall, A. (2013). (Re) considerations of ignorance and resistance in teacher education. *Journal of Teacher Education, 64*(4), 294–304.

Global Challenges Foundation. (2016). Retrieved June 29, 2016, from http://www.globalchallenges.org/reports/Global Catastrophic Risks 2016 Executive Summary.pdf

Laub, D. (1992). Bearing witness or the vicissitudes of listening. In Felman & Laub (Eds,). *Testimony: Crises of witnessing in literature, psychoanalysis, and history*, 57–74. New York, NY: Taylor & Francis.

Lehrer, E., Milton, C. E., & Patterson, M. E. (2011). *Curating difficult knowledge*. New York, NY: Palgrave Macmillan.

Lennon, J. J., & Foley, M. (2000). *Dark tourism*. London: Continuum.

Marcus, A. S. (2005). "It is as it was": Feature film in the history classroom. *The Social Studies, 96*(2), 61–67.

Matthews, S. (2013). 'The trophies of their wars': Affect and encounter at the Canadian War Museum. *Museum Management and Curatorship, 28*(3), 272–287.

Nash, G. (1994). *American odyssey: The United States in the twentieth century.* New York, NY: Glencoe.

Phillips, A. (2002). *Equals.* New York, NY: Basic Books.

Phillips, A. (2014). *Becoming Freud: The making of a psychoanalyst.* New Haven, CT: Yale University Press.

Pitt, A. J. (1998). Qualifying resistance: Some comments on methodological dilemmas. *International Journal of Qualitative Studies in Education, 11*(4), 535–553.

Pitt, A., & Britzman, D. (2003). Speculations on qualities of difficult knowledge in teaching and learning: An experiment in psychoanalytic research. *International Journal of Qualitative Studies in Education, 16*(6), 755–776.

Rothberg, M. (2014). Preface: Beyond Tancred and Clorinda—trauma studies for implicated subjects. In G. Buelens, S. Durrant, & R. Eaglestone (Eds.), *The future of trauma theory: Contemporary literary and cultural criticism* (pp. xi–xviii). New York, NY: Routledge.

Salvio, P. M. (2009). Uncanny exposures: A study of the wartime photojournalism of Lee Miller. *Curriculum Inquiry, 39*(4), 521–536.

Segall, A., & Garrett, H.J. (2013). White teachers talking race. *Teaching Education, 24*(3), 265–291.

Simon, R. I. (2000). The paradoxical practice of zakhor: Memories of "what has never been my fault or my deed." In R. I. Simon, S. Rosenberg, & C. Eppert (Eds.), *Between hope and despair: Pedagogy and the remembrance of historical trauma* (pp. 9–26). New York, NY: Rowman & Littlefield.

Simon, R. I. (2005). *The touch of the past: Remembrance, learning, and ethics.* New York, NY: Palgrave Macmillan.

Simon, R. I. (2011). A shock to thought: Curatorial judgment and the public exhibition of 'difficult knowledge'. *Memory Studies, 4*(4), 432–449.

Simon, R. I. (2014). *A pedagogy of witnessing: Curatorial practice and the pursuit of social justice.* Albany, NY: SUNY Press.

Todd, S. (2001). Guilt, suffering and responsibility. *Journal of Philosophy of Education, 35*(4), 597–614.

Trofanenko, B. M. (2011). On difficult history displayed: The pedagogical challenges of interminable learning. *Museum Management and Curatorship, 26*(5), 481–495.

Trofanenko, B. (2014). Affective emotions: The pedagogical challenges of knowing war. *Review of Education, Pedagogy, and Cultural Studies, 36*(1), 22–39.

Wodtke, L. (2015). A lovely building for difficult knowledge: The architecture of the Canadian Museum for Human Rights. *Review of Education, Pedagogy, and Cultural Studies, 37*(2–3), 207–226.

Zembylas, M. (2014). Theorizing "difficult knowledge" in the aftermath of the "affective turn": Implications for curriculum and pedagogy in handling traumatic representations. *Curriculum Inquiry, 44*(3), 390–412.

Zembylas, M. (2015). *Emotion and traumatic conflict: Reclaiming healing in education.* New York, NY: Oxford University Press.

· 3 ·

TRACES IN NARRATIVES ABOUT
KNOWLEDGE

Evidence, Controversy and Difficult Knowledge

Brendan Nyhan and Jason Reifler are political scientists whose research projects are noteworthy for social studies educators. Their studies (2010; Nyhan *et al.*, 2014) investigate the ways in which factual information can correct misperception or false beliefs in areas such as climate change, the dangers of vaccines, the linking of Iraq with the 2001 attacks on the United States, and other political issues. These issues are of crucial importance in relationship to the ways in which citizens vote to influence policy on matters of consequence. What these studies have consistently found is that facts, in relation to those most consequential domains of thought, do not change our minds about our false or incorrect beliefs. If, though, we were to be corrected on our assumption that people in the UK drive on the right side of the road, we would likely be able to easily change our mind on the matter. However, when issues of import, belief, and identity are at play, people's beliefs and misperceptions simply, and worryingly, do not change. People are, it seems, not likely to have false beliefs corrected by an encounter with disconfirming facts. Nyhan and Reifler (2010) and scientists studying similar patterns demonstrate that this is not exclusive to a particular political ideology. Further, they show how corrections to misperceptions not only fail to change the minds of the study participants, they actually *increase* misperceptions, what is referred to as the "backfire effect." So much for evidence-based decision making.

In her discussion of this emerging body of research, Maria Konnikova (2014) writes that the issues around the ways in which people consistently dismiss corrections to their false beliefs have to do with issues of identity and the ways we think about ourselves rather than issues of under-education or ideology. It may not be surprising that political issues directly related to identity are the kinds of things that people are resistant to changing their minds about. Race, class, gender, and sexual orientation would fall into this category. However, what Nyhan did find helpful in getting people to consider a revision to their thinking were thinking of, and calling attention to, prior instances of self-affirmation where the person was made to feel competent and worthy. Their findings demonstrated that thinking of self-affirming stories in general, not even in particular contexts related to the topic at hand, allowed people to be more open to new information. Being affirmed as a competent person was *the* factor that allowed people the possibility to be open to changing their mind.

What this shows for social studies educators and researchers, in short, is that evidence and facts are, on their own, weak interventions in thinking. However, accounting for the ways in which people encounter those facts, their relation to those facts, and the ways in which they impinge upon basic feelings of worth can aid in peoples' more open engagement with knowledge. The resulting implication is that learning about the world does not occur in absence of our intimate relationship with knowledge that we bring with us and have been accumulating from our very first days.

In social studies, just as in the investigations of political science, the disciplinary practices of historical thinking, social inquiry, and discussions of controversial issues carry deep psychical dynamics. Although the potential of these practices has been well documented in research, the psychical demands of learning—that which makes knowledge potentially difficult—have been less so. Psychic life has an impact on our political, social, and civic selves and our orientation to knowledge as it exists in tense relation to belief and emotion. Life in and among difference places heavy demands on the "lovely knowledge" that we develop while growing up. When we encounter knowledge that runs counter to our already held theories of the ways people and the world operate, we are much more likely to dismiss that information than we are to accommodate it and adjust our views accordingly. We are learners who are conflicted in our learning about conflicting views.

Conflict and controversy are at the center of social studies education (as I elaborate below) and are central features of our own subjective lives. In a psychoanalytic view, the linear chronology of step-by-step stage and development theories gives way to a view of development in which the self is always navigating conflicting pressures, desires, expectations, and our interpretations of them. Rendered psychoanalytically, it is not as though we ever leave the "old" versions of ourselves behind forever, as we move from phase to phase of our lives. Development, Anna Freud writes, is considered here as "new editions of very old conflicts" (*cf.* Britzman, 1998, p. 2). In this way our development is multi-directional, such that "an adult state of mind may be found in the baby: an infant's in the adolescent; a young child's in the old man" (Waddell, 2002, p. 9). An adult can, of course, be seen throwing a fit, an infantile response to what is felt as a social catastrophe or an attack on the self. On the other hand, young children can tolerate adversity and ambiguity in completing a particular task. But these aren't ever stable positions. We never "reach" adulthood once and for all because we will always be revisited by the pressing relations that make up our life in the world. Conflict is central to movements in who were in the most personal and most social ways imaginable.

In social studies education, we tend to worry about the controversy elicited by a particular text, film, or photograph in terms of what the students can handle at a particular phase of their development. However, Britzman (2007) and Gilbert (2014) insist that we remember that the students with whom we work are not the only ones who have personalities and who are moving through an education or development. Our worries about controversy ought to be given attention on their own terms and investigated as to what they signify of the worriers themselves rather than the objects of those worries. We are compelled to remember that teachers too (and researchers, of course) are always working in relation to their own adolescence and childhood. Psychoanalytic views bring into focus the turmoil of such development in which "every move forward in development entails a degree of internal disruption and anxiety which temporarily throws the personality into disarray" (Waddell, 2002, p. 8). Each of these disruptions is relational as well and, therefore, becomes the domain of our social worlds. What we think of as our own individual selves are always in relation to those individuals and structures around us and, also, in relation to investments of who we think we are based on our personal histories. This makes for interesting work in education where the focus on development is usually on the students.

I see social studies lessons in these developmental lurchings. In this chapter I elaborate on the significance of what might be called our "social education" that is acquired through what Elliot Eisner (2001) might call the implicit curriculum of society and what otherwise might be called public pedagogy (Sandlin, Schultz, & Burdick, 2010). In our learning about society and our role within it, we will always be bumping up against the constructed terrain of the social world—its categories, narratives, institutions, and prohibitions. Drawing from a psychoanalytic vantage, I will describe how the ways in which we bump up against those social objects are shaped by our earliest social encounters, which are often with our parents or primary caregivers, and which also give rise to the emotional attachments we have to our ideas about the world. Then, I discuss these difficulties of social studies education in relationship to the most promising practices we have in the field: discussion/deliberation of controversial issues, authentic pedagogical work, and historical inquiry. The difficulties I discuss are intended to add to and complement the ways in which we understand the work of cultivating a classroom space in which students are invited into the complex and uncertain terrain of social life.

Social Studies in/as Relation

Social Studies From the Beginning

Our learning to be in the world with others begins long before we step into a classroom; it begins immediately after we are born. In infancy, the first lesson we learn is our radical dependency on our primary caregivers, followed quickly by the reality that we are separate from them, that they have other things to do besides attend to our every wish, and that there is something called "the world" that doesn't follow the same roads as do our desires. Quickly we are rushed into relationships with others and are forced to negotiate the terms in which we share treasured objects. Our earliest lessons in difference place a forceful demand on our limited, but growing, capacities to engage in the world through language. And because our abilities to communicate are limited and the emotional demands are so strong and insist on being "in" the world somehow, we might have a tantrum, or smash an otherwise beloved object, or we might bite or hit or scratch. We do that for all sorts of reasons, one of which is to see what comes next. We wonder what effect we can have in the world, even if that effect is destructive. If we are lucky, when we are frustrated there will be people around who understand that we aren't adults yet. And, if we are lucky again, they will attend to us and help us learn about the ways in which the world is not organized around our desires as much as we wish that it were. They help us deal with the disappointment or the "insult that the world is not organized around your sovereignty" (Berlant, 2011, p. 85). They might offer us different ways of articulating our frustrations by recognizing them and helping us give language to the problem. They might help us find other things that might approximate the satisfaction of having what we initially wanted. We hope that they leave us with a sense of trust that the world is a place in which our needs can be safely met.

The figure of trust is related to this radical dependency, rooted in infancy and connected to democracy. Psychoanalysts have something to say about the social significance of trust that is forged in our earliest relations. For Erik Erikson (1993), basic trust versus mistrust is the inaugural crisis in a series of crises that mark our lives. When all goes well in early life, we are left with a sense of the world and of others as trustworthy. Trust "is a basic mechanism for handling the demands and dangers of everyday social life" and is "what enables individuals to achieve a practical engagement with the open nature of modern social life" (Elliot, 1994; cf. Frosh, 2001, p. 65). The basic assumption about the world as trustworthy has obvious consequences for the ways that we imagine our relationship to the world. As I will discuss further below, much of the literature in social studies education that forwards the ideas of deliberative democracy, discussion of controversial issues, and authentic intellectual work has an underlying assumption in the ways in which we trust each other to attend to our best attempts at speaking, listening, and responding.

However, as we know, there is a significant amount of mistrust at play in our society—and that is likely a wild understatement. The figure of mistrust on the part of a citizen makes for an entirely different view of the public and a heightened expectation that the others with whom we share communities are out to get us. Throughout history we find instances of a citizenry with an orientation toward mistrust of some Other that influences and substantiates legally sanctioned policy that harms that Other's group. These can be read as symptoms of unresolved (un-recognized) conflicts from earlier situations. Dependence, vulnerability, trust/mistrust are terms that demonstrate "how citizenship itself is constituted in part as a set of fantasy relationships in which individual subjects and their communities are reciprocally entwined" (Frosh, 2001, p. 70). The fantasy relationships in this case are the ways we imagine others to be: safe or unsafe, worthy of protection or worthy of dismissal or violent enactments.

There is, in other words, a large degree of imagination, what psychoanalysts call fantasy, at play in the work of the citizen. These tendencies to imagine how particular ways about particular things are predicated upon, though not determined by, our earliest relationships and are enacted in new situations as we enter into our social lives. In the moments when we learn, in childhood through adulthood, we utilize (at least in part) our infant selves' understandings of the world around us because "when faced with new and familiar events, whatever our age, our time repeats old conflicts" (Britzman, 2007. p. 1). The timeline of development is uneven. We are always bumping up against, and in relationship with, institutions and social conventions into which we struggle to figure out our belonging (or not). For most children, that entry is through the institution of public schools where their social studies education will continue both within and beyond the times in which they open their history books or study world maps. It would be a mistake to not also consider the family a social institution imbued with its own ideological and political complexities. We do, however, go to and learn from school.

However, our radical dependency on others does not end when we leave the nursery. Nor do the social studies lessons get any easier. We will enjoy various successes and failures in group settings, in classrooms and on playgrounds, and at dinner tables, in restaurants and at home. What we experience as success will be either confirmed or challenged in society. If we answer the math question correctly, will our "friends" be happy with us? Will they look the other way? In either case, what will we do to accommodate those reactions? How will we begin to feel our way into our senses of what it means to be "me"? These questions are always, from the very beginning, imbued, shot through, and constituted by others in the world and their own relationships to the culture and society, their codes and narratives and rules, in which they live. Social studies education is the education we never wanted but eternally need in order to sustain our relations in the world.

What I am explaining can help with an understanding of some traditional views and practices of social studies. The view of social studies education as a place where a teacher dispenses knowledge to students about the world, while stereotypical, has a certain resonance with a view of knowledge that psychoanalysts have long understood. That is, as infants, we see our parents or caregivers as all-knowing and in possession of boundless wisdom. One does not need to spend too much time in a social studies (or maybe any class for that matter) to hear a student ask, often with exasperation, "Do we need to know this on the test?" or other questions that presume the role of the teacher as the holder of all worthy knowledge. The implicit demand here (and in other queries about "doing it right" or "well enough") is that the teacher delivers the necessary goods. Students are frustrated by the teacher who interprets this process of teaching and testing and does something other than comply with those students' stated demands. Many students have learned through implicit curriculum that school is important insofar as it can provide a credentialing service for social advancement. Therefore, that demand for test preparation may not be terribly surprising.

Perhaps, though, this is also a trace, an effect, a lingering presence of early relationships to knowledge "which rests on the assumption that the adult knows all there is to be known and that this concrete bundle of knowledge can be taken over by the student as a package. Such a belief leads to a demand that the adult 'hand it over'; 'it' being a body of knowledge, an 'answer, a skill, a 'cure,' or perfect understanding" (Salzberger-Wittenberg & Osborne, 1993, p. 25). Here, this early relation to knowledge plays out as a demand for the exchange of concrete and usable knowledge. This stands in opposition to the view of the teacher as "someone who is concerned to help children to learn and acquire ways of finding out about the world" (*ibid.*). The teacher, of course, can never find out about the world for another person. The relationship between people, the world, and knowledge is something where psychoanalysis provides social studies education in particular with a resource for thinking about what is happening in their work and world. It might help us think about why it is so difficult to put people in positions where the outcome is unknown and uncertainty is prevalent; such experiences run against our earliest, and always familiar, modes of relating to the world.

Our first relationships in the world do not pre-determine our actions in the future. What they do, though, is carry through to our current situations, they help us create narratives and structures that allow us to interpret the world in particular ways. They put us in relationship to social constructs against which our selves are formed. They return again and again, and so although we are no longer infants, nor are our students, we each have our experiences of infancy that serve as a orienting factor toward issues like obedience, safety, authority, trust, and reciprocity. Each of those are, of course, crucial facets of a democracy to consider within the formal disciplinary confines of social studies education.

The Adolescent Social Studies Curriculum

Most of the pre-service and practicing social studies teachers with whom I work are secondary- level teachers and therefore are tasked with teaching adolescents. Just as there are social studies lessons occurring in infancy and in our early experiences with others, adolescents are similarly engaged in a social studies curriculum that exists mostly beyond the confines of what typically counts as the curriculum. The adolescent is up to something. What is it that adolescents are urgently wanting to know? Many of the same dramas that follow us around and beg for our attention began early on, but now they take place on a different stage. For starters, adolescents are engaged in urgent research projects related to living with others. There is the project of consolidating a "me," during which they will over invest in a range of social practice trying to find out how they feel. There is the project of understanding what it means to be sexual as anyone who has spent any time with adolescents will acknowledge.

The adolescent is in somewhat of a bind. They are expected to act like grownups but are treated like children. They have matured sexually but are told to be wary of sexuality. On one hand, adolescence is conceptualized as a psychological stage in which people work out these and other conflicts and carry out a project of "forming a coherent self". In completing such a project, adolescents use other people in their lives, relationships, memories, wishes, fears, senses of safety and experiences of fear or unease. If learning to be in the world with others is provisionally considered as the goal of social studies, then adolescence is that part of the social studies where the fashioning of a "self," a "me," is made from the materials that are the others in their world.

On the other hand, a second view of adolescence is one of a social construction, where scholars note that this stage in life has taken on shifting meanings and has corresponded with the rise of capitalism. It is important to note that adolescence is conceptualized based on historical, cultural, and social contexts. Social studies education ought to take note that the teenagers with whom they work are conceptualized differently across time and space. In all of these conceptualizations, though, the adolescent is a person who is learning to be a self in relation to the world and to others.

As anyone who works in schools with adolescents will likely agree, teenagers can exhibit tumultuous, surprising, and frustrating traits. I think it is important to discuss why that is. One set of reasons can be explained by the behavioral and brain psychologists who will rightly point out that the teenaged brain, like all brains, are under development. In the adolescent years, though, the region of the brain that researchers not for its connection to impulse control is still under significant revision. Adolescents will be observed making risky and impulsive decisions. An implication for teachers arising from this fact of the brain is that wishing or disciplining away that impulsivity is likely an impossible task. This invokes questions about how a social studies educa-tion can operate in relation to learners who are engaged in experiments with authority, power, and identity. Among these is the difficult question: What can adolescents do with rules, then, particularly when those rules are given to being broken through the rebellious tendencies of the teenager?

But another reason teenagers are frustrating and surprising is because some adults characterize them as such. Adolescence is a social construct, but the construct has psychical consequences for the individual moving from child-hood into adulthood. This is to say that the adolescent is always in relation to an adult world who puts particular kinds of social and cultural expectations onto them. Jen Gilbert (2014) is helpful in her articulation of this point:

> If you show me an adolescent, you certainly also show me parents, teachers, friends and peer groups, school, the police, the fashion industry, the media, the mall, and so on. These figures and institutions constitute a facilitating environment for adolescent development or, more particularly, for the adolescent to use as he or she goes about the work of growing up. (p. 34)

The larger social world, that is, constitutes a curricular space in which issues centered in social studies education (identity, culture, politics, difference, and the like) are practiced and experienced in ways that are typically not engaged within formal curricular spaces.

Social studies education can be aided by considering Adam Phillips's (2009) elaboration on teenagers and their relationships to rules. If we con-sider that adolescents are engaged in the project of creating a social "me" in the world, then part of that "me" is the relationship between it and the rules. Schooling often means the demand for compliance, "something the adoles-cent justifiably hates and the teacher feels he or she must demand" (Britzman, 2015, p. 73). Rules are the things we make to demarcate behavior, and we spend a great deal of time invested in the idea that rules ought to be followed, and in many cases they ought to be. However, we also ought to be rather wor-ried if we deliver a generation of adolescents to the adult world who can think of nothing else to do with the rules aside from obey them. Therefore, Phillips (2009) writes, "Adults who look after adolescents have both to want them to behave badly, and to try and stop them; and to be able to do this, adults have to enjoy having truant minds themselves" (p. 16). What he means is that we adults have to enjoy the ways in which whether to break a rule is an open question, and that we are meant to help students in "creating problems—or clarifying what they really are—and not about solving them" (p. 16). Not offering solutions to problems is a pedagogical strategy, one that allows for the practice of living with the ambiguity that the social world provides.

And perhaps the highest stakes test of all is whether, or in what ways, and in which circumstances the adolescent can tolerate that ambiguity as well, a point to which I return below. Adolescence is typified by a desire to have things overly certain. Britzman (2013) sees the risk of adolescence as the temptation to split "knowledge into good or bad; where friends are either loyal or pretenders; where adults are either friend or foe; and where the line between conviction and absolutism blurs" (p. 78). Psychoanalytically inflected notions of learning will invite us to be suspicious when knowledge is offered in the stark terms of this or that, which is often an indication of a defense against thinking more complicated, less comforting thoughts.

If we are to think about the social studies lessons of an adolescent as occasions that the centrality of rules and their fluidity come to the fore, then they are learning the complicated lessons of politics, but mostly these lessons are occurring outside of the classroom. When a youth has to decide whether to go to a party, which one to go to, and with/out which friends, they are engaged in politics. If politics answers the question: what should we do together?, then the political savvy of the teenagers populating our economics or U.S. history classrooms gets a good deal of practice, despite that practice not being specifically called upon in the lesson plan. The social studies lesson is already occurring, students having made the political decision either to comply and satiate the teacher or to defy into a seeming withdrawal from the social studies.

Painful lessons of what happens to ourselves in relation to others are a hallmark of adolescence. We learn that what we say to others and about them when they are not around has consequence. But it is not as though the lessons end there. In adulthood we live with learning about our lives in relationship to others. As I drive to and from my office to write this book, I am radically vulnerable to the scores of drivers with whom I share the road. At any moment I am never farther than a sneeze, a distracted text message, a moment of distraction away from injury. Yes, those roads are paid for by taxes and are thus the location for our civics lesson as well as a scene in which we could recognize the common good. But it is also worthy of a social studies lesson to consider the wonders of us all following rules in order to care for each other in the spaces those roads determine. White and yellow lines, green and red lights. Obeying the wishes of others doesn't always mean that we are being duped by authority. Sometimes we obey out of the consideration for the lives and bodies of people, even those with whom we share communities but who we likely do not know.

All of these social studies lessons shape the ways we act in the world. And, it is not only psychoanalysts who have identified our early experiences in relationships occurring beyond the auspices of "social studies education" as having political consequences for citizenship. Political scientists Marc Hetherington and Jonathan Weiler (2009) found that the ways that people feel about parenting are better predictors of political leanings toward authoritarianism than demographic markers such as gender, income, and education. In order to investigate preferences for authoritarian rule, these researchers asked four questions related to their preferences for how children should behave. Those who preferred children to be obedient, well-behaved, and deferential toward elders rather than self-reliant, curious, and independent were much more likely to have a preference for authoritarianism.

In this view, our home life is still distinct from institutional life but not in the ways we might generally think of it. Our home life, our "private life" cannot be considered as separate from a political life because of the degree to which our relationship to and with authority influences (though cannot predict) how we participate as adults. From the beginning we are moving through a social studies curriculum outside of schools, yet that other social studies education meets the one with which we are familiar in significant ways.

The difficult lessons that we learn as we grow up inside and outside schools constitute a curriculum whereby we are taught about authority, negotiation, politics, and how we generally see ourselves as fitting into the world around us. As the formal curriculum of social studies attempts to add a more sophisticated, formal structure around citizenship education, we are then asked in many ways to forget or ignore those lessons. There are extraordinarily promising pedagogies available to social studies educators, and those strategies enliven these more primary ways of thinking and knowing about the world.

Contestation and Controversy in Social Studies Education

Definitions and articulations of social studies education have been forwarded, fostered, and disputed since the beginning of the field in the early parts of the twentieth century (Evans, 2004; Cherryholmes, 2013). Transmission or transformation, participatory or justice-oriented, disciplinary or postmodern, basic or advanced, social science or reflective inquiry? Scholars have invested heavily in producing models for conceptualizing just what it is that we are and ought to be doing with young people as they learn about social studies. Cherryholmes (2013) explains that such tensions do not stand in the way of social studies education. Rather, they define the field. Rather than trying to make a normative claim about the way that all social studies ought to be conducted, we might be better served understanding the tensions, ambiguities, and uncertainty with which we are all faced. The field is made up of knotted contestations over the grounds that ought to be covered.

These debates occur in a mostly contained way within a modest-sized scholarly field. But social studies is debated in ways that circulate widely as well. Some theoretical stances are deployed against the stated purposes of social studies education to argue for or against particular ways of teaching and learning. That's the category into which this book fits. When social studies is located as a site of public attention, it is often in relationship to debates over the content, the specific "whats" and "whos" of social studies standards. These are widely understood as political arguments between rival factions of a two-party system stuck in a partisan dance. Deep political, emotional, investments are revealed in these public debates about the content and delivery of social studies education. When citizens and their representatives argue over who should be included in the curriculum and how they should be represented, they are arguing about deeply held notions of good, bad, right, wrong, "us," "them," and so on.

Passionate arguments arise about what students should and should not be taught. Worries about knowledge are found again and again in relationship to social studies standards. Legislators and other members of government weigh in on the degree to which a particular historical figure ought to be included in curricula, and if they are included, about the nature of such inclusion. In Texas, for example, the debate is about how Islam is represented, with some feeling that the depictions in textbooks are too sympathetic to Muslims although others consider the representation to be fair (Straus, 2014).

Another example occurred in the spring of 2016 when the state of Georgia was in the process of revising state social studies standards. A member of the state legislature wrote a critique of the proposed standards: "I find no logical reason why President George Washington continues to be omitted from the standards. This should be corrected. He is not mentioned until grade 4, and this is far too late to introduce our most preeminent Founding Father" (Downey, 2016). Although this legislator did not provide a further explanation why grade 4 would be too late for students to be introduced to George

Washington, we can detect worry about the absence of knowledge. One might ask, for example, too late for what? What is it that this elected representative worries about happening if a child does not have a formal lesson addressing Washington's role in the nation's founding? What consequence is the ghosted motivation of such a preoccupation? This concern is found in other debates about the Advanced Placement United States History curriculum, and in 2015 it led a school board member in Colorado to write that it "should promote citizenship, patriotism, essentials and benefits of the free enterprise system, respect for authority and respect for individual rights. Materials should not encourage or condone civil disorder, social strife or disregard of the law" (Ganim, 2015). This is evidence that knowledge is not just a disembodied set of objects subject to neutral exchange. It is evidence that people attach significant meaning to knowledge and invest a great deal into the narratives into which that knowledge fits. This is evidence of earlier relationships to authority, learning, and knowing.

These public controversies imply that some knowledge is so dangerous as to be withheld from children. Within the controversies are thinly veiled references to worries about what happens when students are asked to consider an historical record that includes racial violence, sustained injustice, and attempts at ameliorating that injustice. In these debates we find concrete acknowledgment that we worry about what knowledge will do to people. It is certainly not the case that the more one knows, the better one is. There is something else there. Knowing has an effect. Knowing is affective. Knowledge is dangerous. Anxiety about the consequences of knowledge are part of social studies education. Something more occurs in social studies education than the acquisition of skills to be a citizen because from the very beginning social studies is populated with these and other worries. We are more than collectors of knowledge. We also are resistors to it. We ignore knowledge. We disavow it. We project it. We use it as a weapon. We accommodate it.

All of this controversy is happening and surrounding social studies education before we even consider the practices that occur in classrooms where the most promising strategies researchers advocate also involve contestation. Debate, structured academic controversy, discussion of controversial public issues, historical thinking, and broadly considered inquiry strategies each have students invited into dispute, contestations and dissent. At each of these locations we find the field awash in controversy. Put differently, these features of social studies education reveal controversy, difference, and dissent as centering forces of the field. Further, and relatedly, these arguments represent and reveal deep worries about knowledge in general and how in specific ways knowledge comes to have an effect in the world.

Researchers in social studies education have promising news: Teachers who engage their students in authentic intellectual work are just as likely to see their students succeed on academic measures as those teachers who engage in more traditional rote teaching (Saye & SSIRC, 2013). The same group of researchers substantiate the field's hunch that pedagogies such as Parker's inquiry model yield more complex and sophisticated understandings of social and historical phenomena. Diana Hess and Paula McAvoy (2014) provide further hope in their analysis of what they call "the political classroom." Their research shows the degree to which "complexity and intellectual humility" (p. 53) are both crucial aspects in democratic participation as well as in social studies classrooms. Though they do not draw any casual link between sophisticated practices of discussion and the cultivation of an ability to welcome and tolerate complexity in the classrooms they identify as being the "best," the students are given the space to experience the opportunities to be in the presence of a demand on their beliefs. They have the chance to be confronted with an idea that runs counter to that which they hold dearly. In such situations, not only are students given the opportunity to be good democratic citizens, they are also able to run their own experiments of being in the world by being implicitly asked to wonder: "What do I do with my beliefs in the presence of others"?

For Hess and McAvoy (2014), the political classroom is identified as a location in which issues of public policy are discussed with students via the sound professional pedagogical judgments of a teacher. The purpose of a political classroom has to do with "mastering the ability to talk across political and ideological differences...by teaching students to weigh evidence, consider competing views, form an opinion, articulate that opinion, and respond to those who disagree" (p. 5). Parker (2003) writes similarly about difference, that democracy is predicated upon the presence of "difference and problems" (p. 78). In order to cultivate education spaces in which democratic potentials can be fostered, a particular kind of conversation needs to be cultivated, one that is distinct from "blather" and is called "deliberation" (p. 78). Parker (2008) states "much is learned in deliberation about the problem itself; the alternatives from which a choice must be made; and the other people involved in the discussions, their social perspectives and identities" (p. 76). There is great promise in the discussions and research about the value of deliberation in the cultivation of democratic education.

Hess's seminal work has provided social studies teachers with strategies and models for how controversial issues might be discussed. In addition to her work, several other promising strategies are underwritten by social studies research. For one example, Parker's inquiry model envisions teachers working to set classroom situations where students make hypotheses, consider evidence, and refine their hypotheses as they engage with texts, evidence, and arguments. This is the process that many recognize as crucial to the democratic process, historical investigation, and healthy political discourse. Indeed, the latest articulation of a national social studies curriculum is largely structured around the idea of inquiry. Such strategies are all consonant with qualities of authentic intellectual work that include constructing new understandings about meaningful problems, engaging in evidence-based, disciplined inquiry, and representing those understandings in various modes.

Structured Academic Controversy is another promising strategy that make disagreements the primary object of study (Parker, 2011). Rather than focus on content from history or civics, the focus is put squarely on the ways in which arguments are fashioned in favor of particular viewpoints and students are asked to become fluent in the construction of those viewpoints. Students are aided in grappling with the complexities of social life when disagreement and tension are centered and treated as a persistent feature of living with other people. The SAC presents the opportunity and explicit invitation to change one's mind. At the beginning of an SAC, students are assigned to one of two positions in relation to a controversy. At the end, students "must decide whether to stick to the assigned position they have been defending or abandon it" as they are instructed to "feel free to change your mind" (Parker, 2011, p. 3). Parker acknowledges the binary structure is oversimplified but also makes the strong assertion that such opportunities to rethink, such invitations to try on viewpoints but not be persuaded to keep them, are valuable tools in classrooms focused on the development of a civic space. Educational spaces in which students are made to be apprentices in democratic practice are marked by the need for people to "respect one another's autonomy by engaging in good-faith critical dialogue that includes a willingness to revise their initially preferred policies and practices as a result of deliberation" (Hanson & Howe, 2011, p. 3).

What this research shows, demonstrates, and argues for is the presence of these sophisticated and enlivening practices that help people into their roles as citizens. The research community in social studies education has a broad consensus about the benefits of inquiry, authentic pedagogy, discussion and deliberation, but there is also wide agreement about a more disconcerting finding: Such practices are disappointingly rare.

What Is Going On in a Controversy?

Many things stand in the way of such practices being used more frequently. This has been elaborated elsewhere and is by now, I suspect, not surprising. The list of roadblocks would include the demand to "meet standards" and to have students do well on tests that are themselves privileging of rather simple knowledge. There are critiques about adequate and appropriate preparation from their university teacher education programs. Further, there is a political divisiveness in the United States that leads teachers to avoid controversy because of the degree to which they perceive (rightly or wrongly) that little can come of such us/them thinking as it plays out in classroom debates. Some teachers believe that students are not yet capable of such "higher order thinking." Some teachers think that such practices are the domain of "pie in the sky" university professors and are not the domain of the real-life practices in classrooms. Each of these is, in their own way and in particular contexts, part of the story. However, the kinds of traces we bring with us from those other social studies lessons, those early lessons in relating to the world elaborated above, return to the settings in which people are asked to confront and engage with dissent and controversy. We rely on an ability to rationally consider evidence in our political views, and we seem to have an inability to articulate the dangers of the wish for certainty, final answers, and firm positions.

The discussion I offer does not stand in opposition to what has been described in the research literature or what many people can identify from their experience. Rather, I think, these issues aid in understanding the deeply held personal wishes that may not even be recognized as those that are circulating in classrooms. The traces of knowledge in these narratives about democracy and citizenship have to do with a reliance on a rational model of coming to know about the social world that is insufficient to account for the subjective experience of conflict and controversy.

As I've written above, controversies function as a grounding figure in social studies education. Hess's (2002) field-leading work about discussions of controversial public issues has centered controversy as containing a considerable potential for pedagogy. Controversial public issues, or "unresolved questions of public policy that spark significant disagreement" can be used to frame and direct students' attention as they practice deliberating and discussing and thereby hone their skills in the creation of robust democracy (Hess, 2002, p. 11). But how can we account for these "sparks"? And what makes a controversy so attractive to social studies educators? Of course controversy interests us, but why? And why is it the case that it is avoided? Hess (2009) notes that teachers avoid engaging students in these conversations because they fear "that they are just too politically charged, could upset administrators and parents, or may be emotionally difficult for students in the class with personal experiences related to" the topics at hand (p. 4). Hess concludes her work by arguing for continued focus and professional development of the kinds of sophisticated strategies necessary for discussion, and Parker and Hess (2001) center the need to teach both "with" and "for" discussion. I agree.

Hess's explanation corroborates what I hear in my work with practicing and pre-service social studies teachers—that they worry about parents' reactions if they talk about something that is infused with emotionally charged content. Controversy reveals passionate investments in points of view and ways of being. Controversy emerges because of passionate conflicts between such passionate investments. And further, controversy enlivens our worries about what happens when those passionate attachments are verbalized.

These passionate attachments, their conflicts, and our worries about them are what make controversial conversations so wonderful and also more uncommon than we'd prefer. The controversy is not just calling into question the finer points of a decision or legal issue, it is also calling upon our theories of what happens to knowledge and what can be done with it as learned through our encounters in all sorts of places that are mostly outside of the classroom. It is calling upon our notions of trust, our abilities to stay within tense encounters, and our ability to engage in processes with uncertain outcomes—all things that are likely to incite discomfort. Thus, we are likely to avoid it.

To illustrate this point I will draw on a recent classroom example from my own practice. In class we had read Michelle Alexander's (2012) book *The New Jim Crow: Mass Incarceration in an Age of Colorblindness*. I asked teacher candidates if they would use excerpts from the book to help their own students understand the concept of structural racism to aid in their understanding of current socio-political life. The majority of their responses had to do with reservations about its use, not because of holes in the argument or because they didn't want to engage it, but because they were worried about controversy.

One student, for example, responded that because he had many African American students in his class, and because he was white, he would not feel comfortable discussing the issue of incarceration. He worried that some of the students would have family who were incarcerated and so the issue might feel too close. Another student responded that she worried about what the parents would say if she introduced the arguments and evidence provided in Alexander's book. Yet another articulated that the argument sounded very anti-white and so might offend white students. Many students nodded in agreement. The controversy is routed into worries located in an imagined, fantasized future. We can engage such imaginings.

For example, I find it curious that the parents about whom we fantasize in conversations like these are most often imagined to be conservative activists. The imagined scenario goes something like this: We have students read from Alexander's book; students get excited, and then parents call and question our choices and accuse us of indoctrination. Of course, things like that do happen, but the interesting feature here is that this is the predominant mode of imagining and, importantly, dismissing, the use of a critical historical text. In order to engage their fantasy, I like to tell students that if one of my children were in their class and they were to study the penal system and the teacher did not bring up issues of racial injustice, then I would be the one who was calling. They find that thought a bit more difficult to imagine than the other, even though both are products of the same imagination. It turns out that our imagination is sometimes not too imaginative. Such imaginative scenarios where we pretend to be unqualified or imagine ourselves to fear the retribution of punishing parents are grounded in our emotional vocabularies that we have absorbed in earlier social studies lessons. We want to engage meaningfully with our students, but we realize that engagement brings dangers. Controversy reveals ambivalence.

The ambivalent reactions we have to simply imagining the discussion, much less actually having the discussion, of controversial issues reveals their importance. Phillips (2015) writes that "We are ambivalent. . .about anything and everything that matters to us; indeed, ambivalence is the way we recognize that someone or something has become significant to us" (p. 13). What this means is that teachers' ambivalence about controversial issues arises out of the significant sense that something about controversies might be dangerous. There is simultaneous desire to engage in the discussion and the desire to avoid the uncertainty they bring. Controversy, then, calls into question a persistent narrative that many teachers have about teaching that circulates implicitly in these stories: Teaching should not anger parents; teaching should be safe, and we should be prepared to deal with what happens.

There are good reasons to be ambivalent about engaging controversy in the classroom. Controversies themselves are produced through, and in tension with, dominant ways of thinking about society. The danger we run in social studies education is in forgetting the ways that a controversial public issue is in and of itself a social construction. For an example, we need look no further than the persistent debates in the US about controlling access to guns in light of an ever-growing list of gun-related homicides. On one hand, we could say there is indeed a controversy. People argue that the Second Amendment protects everyone's rights to purchase and wield whatever sort of firearm they prefer. Other people argue that those rights are in need of some limits. Each of these stances finds arguments as part of ready-made preexisting narratives into which their stances fit. Those competing agendas constitute a controversy. However, by calling this issue a controversy it legitimizes the different sides in it. There is not a legitimate argument to be made for unlimited access to guns. By calling it a "controversy," we are in many ways legitimizing a point of view, elevating it to the status of a plausible course of action. Not every issue that is dangerous or unsafe is controversial. Climate change, tobacco use (less so today, of course), and issues of economic (im)mobility, for example, are potentially unsafe because of the expected reactions and passionate attachments people have to a particular position. But the positions are not equally worthy given the evidence that is available. Naming and legitimizing a controversy allow an individual to externalize the tension of grappling with an issue.

Sometimes ideas simply make us nervous. Just as my examples above elaborate on discussions of race, Hanson and Howe (2011) assert the importance of politicization deliberation in civics classrooms even though it "may not be an easy or comfortable task for teachers" (p. 3). This discomfort has a presence in, but does not hold the focus of, much of the research that is conducted in terms of political discussions, discussions of controversial issues, deliberation, and the like. I'll now focus on two features that are perhaps helpful in considering the experience of conflict or controversy in social studies classrooms: the ability to tolerate uncertainty and the attention to the limits of rational considerations of evidence.

The Evidence of the Insufficiency of Evidence

Despite the difficulties elaborated above, the evidence points in favor of teachers' use of authentic pedagogies. But evidence does a lot of things. The evidence points to climate change being accelerated through our actions, yet we mostly persist in the same actions. The evidence about the correlation between the availability of guns and the increasing incidence of gun violence does little to change the policy landscape around gun legislation. Evidence, then, operates in ways outside of adding wisdom to our decision-making processes

One of the underlying assumptions of the ambitious pedagogies involved in discussion and deliberation includes the reliance on evidence. Students encounter a text, then consider the evidence offered therein, and then they make arguments based on this evidence for or against a particular point of view or course of action. Much of the literature in social studies education is grounded in similar practices like the ones described above. In order to think like an historian, you parse through evidence in a rational process by which you arrive at a best answer. In order to arrive at an informed position on a public policy issue, you look at the evidence supporting various positions and make a rational argument supporting your viewpoint on that issue.

Journalist Shankar Vedantam (2010) writes that most of what we think about the way people act is based on a similar theory, which holds "that human behavior [is] the product of knowledge and conscious intention" (p. 5). The past twenty years or so, though, has yielded a tremendous amount of research showing how this is, simply, not the case. Marshall Alcorn (2013) puts it this way:

> People are often, and for various reasons, resistant to taking information that, though it solves real practical problems, conflicts with their identities and their key values. Under such conditions people deny the truth or accommodate it through suffering and sacrifice. They do not abandon beliefs called into question by factual information; they resist modes of reason that threaten their identities. (p. 46)

Alcorn highlights a part of our thinking apparatus that is predisposed toward protecting already-held beliefs, that lovely knowledge, even when the evidence is stacked against those beliefs. Further, as Alcorn notes,

> We notice peoples' inability to take information, but we keep faith in the transformative value of information itself. In response to encounters with the denial of facts, people do not come to understand that humans do not take in facts. Instead they seek to more urgently produce and publish facts. We see people not taking in facts, and our response is simply to insist more emphatically upon the facts. (p. 22)

What Alcorn is noticing here is the problematic relationship between facts, reason, and belief. The argument he forwards, and one that is of great consequence to social studies teachers who pursue the difficult work of dialogue and deliberation, is that learning the facts carries with it an emotional demand, one that can shut down learning if we are unprepared to allow that emotional current to be part of our classroom life. Alcorn points us to a consideration that the processes by which we inquire into the world involve, in a significant way, an inquiry into our beliefs and that the work of learning is a significant emotional task. And the beliefs or emotional movements may not even be conscious. Of course it is not always difficult to take in new information. A weather report might change our minds about what to wear on a particular day. But when information—good, factual, "evidence-based," clear—is presented to people that runs against what they desire to believe, or believe to be desirable, things get quite a bit more interesting. Mostly the difficulties emerge more clearly the more consequential the information is. And what is perhaps even more disquieting is that is not just a problem for those who are uninformed or uneducated as we might imagine. Rather, there is some research that shows that the more one knows, the more expert a person a is on a particular field or subject, the less likely it is that that person would be open to consider discomforting facts.

So why is evidence a weak intervention? Evidence, and our reliance on it, is a weak intervention because "standard cognitive/rational models do not appropriately account for affect in the evaluation and decision-making process" (Redlawsk, Civettini, & Emmerson, 2010, p. 565). In the previous chapter I discussed how the encounter with others' pain can elicit our own. But in the political realm in which controversies circulate, our deliberative and discussion-based models seem to negate the role of affect, emotion, and experience. Knowledge can trouble our senses. Knowledge is experienced as affect prior to the ability to engage it in on a cognitive level (p. 567). As it relates to the situation of difficult knowledge and the ways in which crises are part of it, affect and new ideas come to us in surprising ways. The various crises are not just in the past, they are also in the present and can be anticipated as inevitably coming in the future. Simply put, as Alcorn (2013) writes, people "do not abandon beliefs called into question by factual information; they resist modes of reasoning that threaten their identities" (p. 46) and they do so in many interesting ways.

Processes of acknowledging the emotional valence of social thought have been described as "the backfire effect," "motivated intelligence," and "confirmation bias" in various communities of political science and psychology. Each of these terms from diverse fields of study, not just in psychoanalysis, recognizes what I've outlined above, which is that there are other things that people are compelled to do with encounters with knowledge beyond rational consideration thereof. Psychoanalysts do, though, have a particular vocabulary to describe this process including the idea of resistance described in the previous chapter and the related idea of ignorance, which I will describe briefly here as it relates to learning and also to social studies more specifically.

Part of the reason why evidence is not used is a function people have that Alcorn (2013) calls "the desire not to know," what psychoanalysts identify as processes of resistance, ignorance, or disavowal. Much of the time when we think about ignorance, we use the term to reference the uneducated and uninformed. This kind of ignorance ought to be addressed in any social studies curriculum. Social studies educators may also be invited to think about ignorance in the more psychoanalytic rendering of the terms.

Ignorance as Evidence

Ignorance in that sense is less about what is not present and more about what has been forgotten. In this sense of ignorance the process begins with an encounter between an individual and some experience or knowledge in which that thing is "ignored." To ignore something is not an absence of knowledge, it is more of a refusal of that knowledge because of the potential consequences that knowledge can have (Felman, 1982).

Ignorance has a function in the social studies because of the ways we (teachers and students) can simultaneously know and then refuse particular social realities. Ignorance is related to social processes that challenge deeply held ways of understanding how the world works. Related to the above example about teaching race and incarceration, ignorance could be said to be functioning in the ways that teaching simultaneously acknowledge the problem but then retreat from engaging with it. This is not a resistance as we might normally think of it, as though a student is directly telling a teacher that she wishes to not know the lesson. Rather, it is a resistance that might, in fact, look more like learning that its opposite. Students do well in classes, appear to be paying attention and indeed are, and can even do well on the tests. Yet, after the semester is over, learners in that course, the successful ones, will revert back to their own prior versions of the learning (see Alcorn, 2013). Resistances and ignorance can often be more like a compromise that learners make in order to keep up appearances rather than risk breakdowns in meaning that accompany significant learning (Garrett & Segall, 2013; Segall & Garrett, 2013).

den Heyer and Abbott (2011) extend ignorance directly into social studies education with their term "privilege-ignorance nexus" (p. 8). For these scholars, ignorance is a socially constructed result of a pedagogy that sanctions particular ways of knowing and, significantly, not-knowing. The privilege-ignorance nexus is a product of discourses and practices that perpetuate narratives which obscure the lives and experiences of those already disadvantaged. If people are in the condition of ignorance because of a life in poverty and the ways in which these people struggle to live, it is inextricably linked to privilege. They view teacher education as a location in which there exists "the necessity to learn from knowledge already possessed and to learn from resistance to questions, issues, or alternative perspective that potentially put at risk what (and on what basis) we claim to know" (p. 10). Resistance and the ways in which we experience the anxieties around knowledge, scholars suggest, become objects of study in the curriculum.

Finally, ignorance functions in social studies education in at least one additional way, through the systematic and intentional production thereof. The field of science studies has given rise to the term "agnotology" to denote the cultural construction of ignorance (Proctor & Schiebinger, 2008). The study of the construction of ignorance, agnotology takes its grounding point in fields of misinformation in the political realm. For instance, agnotologists have demonstrated clearly the ways in which political operatives, think-tanks, and corporate actors all conspire to construct doubt in relationship to anthropogenic climate change. The very presence of climate change as controversy is a cultural construct. It is, in fact, not a controversy until vast amounts of money and public relations experts were deployed to introduce doubt about its truth. Through Wikileaks and Edward Snowden, we also know that we are intentionally kept ignorant about various activities of our democratically elected government. In this sense the social studies is a prolonged engagement with ignorance along the three axes of absence, unconscious defense, and conscious construction.

Each of these dynamic features figures into the difficulties of deliberating a controversial issue. Students might need to do more; the consideration of other perspectives may pose an epistemological or psychic threat, and, indeed, the very nature of the controversy may be a total farce to begin with. Psychoanalysts teach us that although we presume, and operate on the presumption, that knowledge is desired and makes things better, a lot of knowledge can bring discomfort and pain. And, further complicating this situation, we tend to defend ourselves against just such discomfort. This is not just a psychoanalytic "truth." Social psychologists confirm this, too. Medical practitioners observe this phenomenon regularly, as well, as they see patients who despite "knowing" that particular behaviors are bad for them, continue to carry out those same behaviors. Similarly, in social studies education research we demonstrate again and again how particular pedagogies yield the most promise, yet those practices are not taken up in the classroom.

Conflict and Tolerating Uncertainty

Perhaps another reason why controversial discussions are not more common in social studies classrooms is related to the idea that evidence has a much heavier emotional burden than normally thought. Evidence that counters belief is felt as an affective force before our cognitive or rational apparatus begins its work because that evidence induces conflict. Psychoanalysis is built on a theory of conflict between competing parts of the self that are in ongoing tension. Subjective life cannot exist without conflict, and as such psychoanalytic ways of thinking propose a kind of "multiple self" where desires are pressured into various modes of expression through the circuits of society's rules and demands (Freud, 1968). This conflict is the foundation of our subjective and conscious experience of the world. Even if we were to think about this conflict as "interior," we would also have to acknowledge that the tensions are at least partly based on what we interpret as social expectations of a particular situation.

I contend that social significance can be made from the very fact of such discomfort and the conflict to which it relates. Discomfort signifies; it alerts us to events going on around us that conflict is necessary in democracy and, therefore, might be considered as part and parcel to social studies education and not only in terms of solving it. Put a little differently, conflict is encouraged in democracies at the same time conflict makes us nervous. "Psychoanalysis," Adam Phillips (2009) writes, "like democracy, works through the encouragement and validation of new forms of association and the conflicts they inevitably reveal" (p. 21). Conflict in this view is a novel idea, and what is occurring in the discussions of controversy in classrooms is, at least in part, the encouragement to make new associations between old objects of knowledge.

What a psychoanalytic view offers social studies educators is an invitation to resist the resolution of that ambivalence and instead learn to tolerate uncertainty and ambiguity. Keats (1817) has termed this ability "negative capability," the ability to be "capable of being in uncertainties, mysteries, doubts, without any irritable reaching after fact and reason." This ability has something to do with the idea that confronting uncertainty can tempt us toward closing down thought by finding a position in which to stand and to which we can commit with resolute certainty. Resolute certainty is viewed suspiciously because of how it would serve as an impediment to thinking about things anew. If we already think we have the answer, we are less likely to ask the question again. In a democracy in which participation demands the thoughtful engagement with novel situations where people disagree, the positioning of certainty ought to be in the background. In the foreground should be curiosity and propositional forms of experiments with ways of knowing and acting in the world.

The ability to tolerate ambiguity correlates with history education researcher Lisa Farley's (2009) formulation that "uncertainty is the very ground of meaning making, not its opposite" (p. 551). What being able to tolerate uncertainty and stay within an experience of ambiguity does is to "help people find new ways to address change and the resistances or blockages to change" (French, 2001, p. 480). Elizabeth Ellsworth (2005) brings this idea to pedagogy by referencing the benefits of a refusal of certainty in learning, suggesting an ethical commitment to a refusal "of the last word or to presume to know that last word. . .a refusal of the heroic position of mastery" (p. 114). The kind of democratic practice that social studies teachers and researchers are after via the use of discussion and deliberation requires that individuals are able to maintain such a position, at least for a time. Each of these scholars and stances capitalizes on the psychoanalytic practice of resistance to offering definitive answers in favor of an ongoing experiment with who we are and what we think.

Social studies education requires the ability to tolerate ambiguity because democracy is a process in which no outcomes are guaranteed in advance. In deliberations we cannot know what will be said ahead of time. Part of what teachers need to be able to do is understand that unpredictability and uncertainty, while perhaps initially uncomfortable, are part of the difficulty of teaching but also that which holds the most promise. An obvious part of discussion or deliberation is going to be the existence of uncertainty because, at least we hope, competing views and positions will be circulating so that each have purchase on our thinking.

One way I remember working with high school students and helping them into murky territory occurred during a project in which I had them analyze and respond to then president George W. Bush's tax policies. I provided two sets of information purportedly showing accurate information about the tax plans, one was from the White House and the other was from a tax policy analysis non-profit group. The two sets of data analyzed the same tax policies and, as you might expect, had diametrically opposing arguments about the anticipated effects thereof. The document from the White House said that the plan would benefit middle-class income earners; the document from the tax policy non-profit group used the same plan and concluded/argued that it would devastate the middle class. Students would read these documents, and though it took a while, they began to realize the problem. They would ask me, "Which one is right?" My reply was always the same: "Exactly."

That reply frustrated many students, but it put them in the position to understand that knowledge is something other than a part of an arsenal to deploy against a certain reality. And it put them in a different relation to a teacher as being someone else than the person who controls the flow of that arsenal of knowledge. Knowledge was related to perspective, and such a relationship marked a different kind of emotional engagement because it implicated the learner in their own experience of coming to know, one in which the question was privileged over the answer.

Social Studies and the Loss of Lovely Knowledge

The C3 (NCSS, 2013) framework states that a productive civic life is dependent upon being aware of changing cultural and physical environments; knowing the past; reading, writing, and thinking deeply and acting in ways that promote the common good. The goals of a social studies education include the development of "clear and disciplined thinking" (p. 6) that will help them in their college, career, and civic life. The contributions to be made in these areas, in their specificity, are left to the imagination in most cases. What ought to occur in college, career, and civic life is not discussed. Social studies education is stated as a way to get young people ready to do other things. Rendered in this way, social studies education is a process of helping people know the "right stuff" that one needs to know in order to make a "good" decision. In all cases this assumes a rational actor which, as I have elaborated above, may often be a problematic assumption.

Nevertheless, the decisions that are referenced in position statements for social studies education like the C3 frameworks and the NCSS goals assume a particular kind of relation between individuals. Individuals are connected through their public lives, and while little specific language is devoted to how one might relate to another, there is a focus on respect, perspective taking, and rational argumentation. This would mean that who we are to each other, as it relates to the social or political fabric, the democratic goal, is (ideally) a result of rational deliberation. What I have tried to offer in this chapter is that a "disciplinary" and "rational" view is a limiting one, one that avoids the complications of human subjectivity, relationality, politics, sociality, and community. Put differently, we are at risk of holding a view of learning that often does not hold.

Of course, there are plenty of advantages to rationality and disciplined thinking, but reasoned political discourse is sorely missing. Indeed, it is nearly impossible to find good "role models" for intellectually engaged exchanges about the most pressing topics of our times on most media outlets. I am not suggesting that we disavow the pressing need to critically engage with arguments and evidence. Once issues of society, democracy, and the common good are introduced, though, much more ought to be considered. This is because who we are to each other is always going to be more than a simple exchange of dispassionate viewpoints (however passionately argued they may be). Citizenship is made from conflict. And the conflict is not just between competing views "out there." The competition and conflict are also already on the inside, built out of the earliest relationships we've ever had. As Stephen Frosh (2001) writes, "Citizenship can only be a compromise, a balance between what one might 'truly' desire (to explode all possible constraints) and the limits of what can be allowed if life is to go on" (p. 65). Psychoanalytic considerations allow us to take account of those desires and the necessary changes to those desires that take place in order for society to exist.

As I have mentioned, difficult knowledge is not just the study of violent or traumatic histories. Yes, it acknowledges that it may be difficult for a learner to tolerate such learning. But difficult knowledge also points to the need to "risk approaching the internal conflicts" the learner brings to learning. It is also the "traces in narratives about knowledge" (Pitt & Britzman, 2003, p. 757). Here is where difficult knowledge as a psychoanalytic term that situates a pedagogical experience differs from accounts such as "historical empathy" or the study of "difficult histories" that do not explicitly employ a psychoanalytic vocabulary or understanding. The internal conflicts that Britzman references are the fantasies, reversals, projections, and other defense mechanisms that indicate any individual's ambivalence to knowledge. And these relations to knowledge, while perhaps circulating constantly, are brought into sharp relief within the constraints of learning about terrible histories of violence and loss. But they are present in many other ways in social studies and teacher education.

For starters, calling these conflicts "internal" does not adequately represent the ways in which they are socially produced from the outset. Very little separates the internal world from the external social world. Each one is made out of the other. Those terms of internal and external life may serve us well in order to distinguish and demarcate ourselves as separate entities from others, but we should always be careful to not make the distinctions terribly consequential. An "internal conflict" is, in this context, an artifact of prior social relationships that comes to have a felt impact on the ways that learning is supposed to happen in a particular moment. These fantasies and projections are the crystalized, but never static, residuals of the relationships we've had all along. If we have been in situations that have allowed us to make mistakes without severe repercussions, we may be more likely to try out a new idea in a classroom. Of course, nothing is ever so neat and clean, and so maybe our being allowed to make mistakes has created a situation in which that is all we ever do. Internal conflicts do not lend themselves to such easy plot lines.

The plot lines that are followed in history education, those that are so filled with murder and conquest, are often presented easily as though events were inevitable and causes make effects. Part of what makes difficult knowledge so difficult is that we can't really say, for once and for all, why Hitler rose to power and how it came to be that so many million people were made to suffer and die in the relatively open view of the world. We similarly cannot with full certainty or completeness say what led people to enslave, to lynch, to bomb, to execute other people in any time or place. Difficult knowledge has us grapple with the idea that thinking about "complete knowledge" of anything is an impossible fantasy. The acknowledgment of knowledge's incompleteness marks a pedagogical hinging point for thinking about difficult knowledge. But there is conflict about what we know about the world long before we get to the classroom, and even when we are in classrooms much more is occurring than an essential question and benchmark.

Conclusions

Acknowledging these difficult complications can simultaneously enrich classroom life and expand our understandings of social phenomena and social life. "World making requires self-knowledge of what the world might symbolize or represent for the self" (Britzman, 2000, p. 202). When viewed psychoanalytically, the first acknowledgment is that knowing ourselves is an impossibility due to the fact of our defended selves. Simply put, there are parts of who we are that function beyond our awareness but are simultaneously not a mystery to others. When we introduce an Other into our lives, that person is never just that person alone, because as we interact with Others, we bring to those encounters the experiences, memories, and kinds of educated modes of interaction from our histories of being in the world.

Whether or not researchers and teachers take on an activist stance, all of us are trying to change people's minds in some capacity. Whether it is projects of education for social justice or attempts to become disciplinary experts with pedagogical content knowledge to engage in "best practices," we hope that students will become "good citizens" or "good teachers." We are all hoping in some sense that we are able to influence the thinking of those people with whom we work. But as Alcorn (2013) writes,

> Changes in subjectivity take place in a temporal horizon where a play of thought can have structuring effects on an embodied history of attachment, fear, hope, and security. This prolonged temporal adjustment to new information is perhaps, more than anything else, an exercise in increasing a tolerance for anxiety. (p. 123)

What this means, I think, for teacher education is something that is not too radical, which is that a teacher's education occurs before and after a teacher education program. And in social studies education, learning about the world can bewilder us in the face of its enormity and its feeling of being beyond to such a degree that we would sooner turn away than think further. Can we think of a social studies education whose goal is to aid in an increasing tolerance for anxiety and ambiguity?

I am not suggesting replacing any one agenda with any other agenda or stance. Holding ideas as something other than replacements for each other is something to practice, and it does take a tolerance for anxiety, uncertainty and ambivalence. And it's at this point where I feel like psychoanalysis comes back into the foreground. We can say that teaching is emotionally demanding but that only gets a foot in the door. In a pedagogical relation, what is it exactly that can aid in such an exercise and go further than replay the dance of information provision? How is it that we can offer an intervening picture of what it means to be a teacher (or citizen, or voter, or neighbor), one that balances the view of learning as knowledge exchanging hands with the view that what a good teacher is actually good at is

> stimulating curiosity, making the student more aware of questions to be asked and helping the student to observe the phenomena that are available to his senses, and assisting him to sort such impressions against some framework of understanding. (Salzberger-Wittenberg & Osborne, 1993, p. 26).

The ways in which we relate to the facts of our resistance to facts, our predisposition toward comfort, and a realization of the indeterminacy of learning are the relations of difficult knowledge. Accounting for controversy and enlivened debates are scenes in which citizenship is made out of intimate connections to, and experiences with, authority, knowledge and theories of being in the world with others.

References

Alcorn, M. W. (2013). *Resistance to Learning: Overcoming the desire-not-to-know in classroom teaching*. New York, NY: Palgrave Macmillan.

Alexander, M. (2012). *The new Jim Crow: Mass incarceration in the age of colorblindness*. New York, NY: The New Press.

Berlant, L. G. (2011). *Cruel optimism*. Durham, NC: Duke University Press.

Britzman, D. P. (1998). *Lost subjects, contested objects: Toward a psychoanalytic inquiry of learning*: Albany, NY: SUNY Press.

Britzman, D. P. (2007). Teacher education as uneven development: Toward a psychology of uncertainty. *International Journal of Leadership in Education, 10*(1), 1–12.

Brtizman, D.P. (2015). *A psychoanalyst in the classroom: On the human condition of education*. Albany, NY: SUNY Press.

Cherryholmes, C. H. (2013). What to teach? *Theory & Research in Social Education, 41*(4), 566–574.

den Heyer, K., & Abbott, L. (2011). Reverberating echoes: Challenging teacher candidates to tell and learn from entwined narrations of Canadian history. *Curriculum Inquiry, 41*(5), 610–635.

Downey, M. (2016, March 28). Social studies teachers: Politicians influencing new standards more than educators [Web log post]. Retrieved from http://getschooled.blog.myajc.com/2016/03/28/social-studies-teachers-politicians-influencing-new-standards-more-than-educators/

Eisner, E. W. (2001). *The educational imagination: On the design and evaluation of school programs* (3rd. ed.). Upper Saddle River, NJ: Pearson.

Ellsworth, E. (2005). *Places of learning: Media, architecture, pedagogy*. New York, NY: Routledge.

Erikson, E. H. (1993). *Childhood and society*. New York, NY: W.W. Norton & Company.

Evans, R. W. (2004). *The social studies wars: What should we teach the children?* New York, NY: Teachers College Press.

Farley, L. (2009). Radical hope: Or, the problem of uncertainty in history education. *Curriculum Inquiry, 39*(4), 537–554.

Felman, S. (1982). Psychoanalysis and education: Teaching terminable and interminable. *Yale French Studies* (63), 21–44.

French, R. (2001). "Negative capability": Managing the confusing uncertainties of change. *Journal of Organizational Change Management, 14*(5), 480–492.

Freud, S. (1968). *Civilization and its discontents* (J. Strachey, Ed.). New York, NY: W.W. Norton & Company, Inc.

Frosh, S. (2001). Psychoanalysis, identity and citizenship. In N. Stevenson (Ed.), *Culture and citizenship* (pp. 62–73). London: Sage.

Ganim, S. (2015, February 24). Making history: Battles brew over alleged bias in Advanced Placement standards [Web log post]. Retrieved from http://www.cnn.com/2015/02/20/us/ap-history-framework-fight/

Garrett, H. J., & Segall, A. (2013). (Re) considerations of ignorance and resistance in teacher education. *Journal of Teacher Education, 64*(4), 294–304.

Gilbert, J. (2014). *Sexuality in school*: Minneapolis: University of Minnesota Press.

Hanson, J. S., & Howe, K. (2011). The potential for deliberative democratic civic education. *Democracy and Education, 19*(2), 3.

Hess, D. E. (2002). Discussing controversial public issues in secondary social studies classrooms: Learning from skilled teachers. *Theory & Research in Social Education, 30*(1), 10–41.

Hess, D. E. (2009). *Controversy in the classroom: The democratic power of discussion*. New York, NY: Routledge.

Hess, D. E., & McAvoy, P. (2014). *The political classroom: Evidence and ethics in democratic education*. New York, NY: Routledge.

Hetherington, M. J., & Weiler, J. D. (2009). *Authoritarianism and polarization in American politics*. New York, NY: Cambridge University Press.

Keats, J. (1817). Letter to George and Thomas Keats. *December, 21*(27), 1817.

Konnikova, M. (2014). I don't want to be right. *New Yorker Online*.

National Council for the Social Studies (NCSS). (2013). *The college, career, and civic life (C3) framework for social studies state standards: Guidance for enhancing the rigor of k-12 civics, economics, geography, and history* (Silver Spring, MD: NCSS).

Nyhan, B., & Reifler, J. (2010). When corrections fail: The persistence of political misperceptions. *Political Behavior, 32*(2), 303–330.

Nyhan, B., Reifler, J., Richey, S., & Freed, G. L. (2014). Effective messages in vaccine promotion: A randomized trial. *Pediatrics, 133*(4), e835–e842.

Parker, W. (2003). *Teaching democracy: Unity and diversity in public life*. New York, NY: Teachers College Press.

Parker, W. (2008). Knowing and doing in democratic citizenship education. In L. S. Levstik & C. A. Tyson (Eds.), *The handbook of research in social studies education* (pp. 65–80). New York, NY: Routledge.

Parker, W. (2011). Feel free to change your mind. A response to "The potential for deliberative democratic civic education." *Democracy and Education, 19*(2), 9.

Parker, W. C., & Hess, D. (2001). Teaching with and for discussion. *Teaching and Teacher Education, 17*(3), 273–289.

Phillips, A. (2009). In praise of difficult children. *London Review of Books, 31*(3), 16.

Phillips, A. (2002). *Equals*. New York, NY: Basic books.

Phillips, A. (2015). Against self-criticism. *London Review of Books, 37*(5), 13–16.

Pitt, A., & Britzman, D. (2003). Speculations on qualities of difficult knowledge in teaching and learning: An experiment in psychoanalytic research. *Qualitative Studies in Education, 16*(6), 755–776.

Proctor, R., & Schiebinger, L. L. (2008). *Agnotology: The making and unmaking of ignorance*. Stanford, CA: Stanford University Press.

Redlawsk, D. P., Civettini, A. J., & Emmerson, K. M. (2010). The affective tipping point: Do motivated reasoners ever "get it"? *Political Psychology, 31*(4), 563–593.

Salzberger-Wittenberg, I., & Osborne, E. L. (1993). *The emotional experience of learning and teaching*. London: Karnac Books.

Sandlin, J. A., Schultz, B. D., & Burdick, J. (2010). *Handbook of public pedagogy: Education and learning beyond schooling*. New York, NY: Routledge.

Saye, J., & Collaborative, S. S. I. R. C. (2013). Authentic pedagogy: Its presence in social studies classrooms and relationship to student performance on state-mandated tests. *Theory & Research in Social Education, 41*(1), 89–132.

Segall, A., & Garrett, H.J. (2013). White teachers talking race. *Teaching Education, 24*(3), 265–291.

Straus, V. (2014, November 21). Texas approves social studies textbooks criticized and inaccurate and biased [Web log post]. Retrieved from https://www.washingtonpost.com/news/answer-sheet/wp/2014/11/21/texas-approves-social-studies-textbooks-criticized-as-inaccurate-and-biased/?tid=a_inl

Vedantam, S. (2010). *The hidden brain: How our unconscious minds elect presidents, control markets, wage wars, and save our lives*. Random House Digital, Inc.

Waddell, M. (2002). *Inside lives: Psychoanalysis and the growth of the personality*. London: Karnac Books.

· 4 ·

MOVEMENTS OF DIFFICULT KNOWLEDGE

Hours later, still in the difficulty of what it is to be, just like that, inside it, standing there,
maybe wading, maybe waving, standing where the deep waters of everything backed up, one
said, climbing over bodies, one said, stranded on a roof, one said, trapped in the building,
and in the difficulty, nobody coming and still someone saying, who could see it coming, the
difficulty of that.

He said, I don't know what the water wanted. It wanted to show you no one would come.
                                                                    —Claudia Rankine (2015, p. 83).

Claudia Rankine's (2015) *Citizen: An American Lyric* contains the above epi-
graph, a burst of lyric poetry constructed from CNN footage during August of
2005, the awful time of post-Katrina New Orleans. A defining and troubling
feature of this place and time is the fact that although the hurricane itself
might be called a natural disaster, what one learns is that such strife was in
most every way unnatural. In Rankine's poem we can read the difficulty in
terms of the encounter with trauma, crisis, and vulnerability and how, to the
narrator, the tragic experiences were teaching a lesson.

This chapter presents a group of social studies teachers as they navigate
the terrain of an encounter with a film containing elements of social upheaval, loss, vulnerability, trauma, and crisis—elements that are likely to set the
scene for a situation of difficult knowledge. Although our most "popular" cases

of social trauma are codified in the social studies curriculum while dealing with the Holocaust and slavery, in this investigation I wanted to find out what might happen when the difficult knowledge was "closer" in time and distance to the study participants. How would the five social studies teachers with whom I spoke react to the traumatic representations in Spike Lee's 2006 documentary *When the Levees Broke: A Requiem in Four Acts* (*WTLB*), a film that not only portrays loss, sadness, death, and devastation but also implicates issues of race, politics and other social issues in its telling? Employing a methodology that deployed the psychoanalytic ideas that underwrite and give fuel to the concept of difficult knowledge, I wondered about the ways that knowledge is accepted, refused, welcomed, rejected, mediated, and circulated as individuals are confronted with what are portrayed as unjust events in the social world? I further wondered about the processes that are evident in the talk of individuals about difficult knowledge and how those processes might illuminate different features of our work as social studies teachers.

The confrontation with representations of death, loss, absence, and suffering, followed by a problem with interpretation in which the problem makes another turn toward pedagogy is confounding but demarcates a problem space for teachers and teacher educators who are tasked with educating others about the social world. If learning about the most terrible parts of human history were not difficult already, then the difficulty is reordered and made more complex by the demand to make it the stuff of a lesson plan. Psychoanalytic ways of thinking about such a situation would point to the ways that defenses operate in encounters with the world.

Defense Mechanisms

The notion of defenses is predicated upon the existence of the unconscious and a defended subjectivity. That is, a subject cannot know him/herself in a complete and/or truthful way. The subject will be defended from discomfort and anxiety through the use of what Anna Freud codified as "ego defense mechanisms." Freud (1935/1979) formulates the basis upon which psychoanalysts first understood "ego defenses" as follows:

> When repudiating the claims of the instinct, its [the ego's] first task must always be to come to terms with these affects. Love, longing, jealousy, mortification, pain, and mourning accompany sexual wishes; hatred, anger, and rage accompany the impulse of aggression; if the instinctual demands with which they are associated are to be

warded off, these affects must submit to all the various measures to which the ego resorts in its effort to master them, i.e., they must undergo a metamorphosis. (p. 32)

These affects, as Freud describes them, need to be warded off by the ego (the self) because of the degree to which they are felt as frightening or threatening. Anna Freud codified several defenses, among them: denial, displacement, repression, sublimation, rationalization, regression, and intellectualization. The idea is that the psyche has at its disposal several strategies allowing the metamorphosis of unwelcome affect to proceed. It might happen that a lesson plan fails miserably. A teacher may have spent several hours coming up with resources and designing an activity, but the activity may be flawed and the lesson may instantiate acute frustration. Yet teachers may project the idea of their own fallibility onto their students, who "didn't follow directions" or "were too apathetic to get it" (these are examples from my own history of teaching). A teacher might rationalize a poor lesson by saying something like, "Well, it was just after lunch and students weren't ready to focus." A teacher might deny that a lesson went poorly all together, particularly in the case of being observed and evaluated ("No, the lesson went well!").

The point is not that statements like these are not true, as there is probably a great deal of truth to them. There is no way to be able to say for certain when or where defenses manifest themselves. For psychoanalytic theory, one would only maintain that they do manifest themselves, and we can gain material for interpretation by looking for the places where knowledge comes from, where explanations begin and end, to whom fault is ascribed, and from whom pleasure is derived. The opportunity for teachers to wonder about, rather than assign meaning to, the ways that students react, participate, or engage is enriched by such a psychoanalytic vocabulary in that it invites everyone to hold ourselves open to new possibilities. It acknowledges a world of knowledge and meaning that is always in flux, filled with contradiction, and influenced by things that we simply cannot see for ourselves. This chapter conceptualizes those movements, the metamorphosis of psychic energy vis-à-vis ego defense mechanisms, as the routing and re-routing of difficult knowledge.

Is there a Psychoanalytic Research Methodology?

Early in 2009 scientists had quite a difficult problem as they were trying to figure out whether the moon contained traces of water—and, perhaps, traces of life. Water on the moon, scientists thought, was a distinct possibility, but they could not observe it directly. Any water there is not accessible to researchers in a direct way. There isn't a lake they can see. There exists insufficient funding or public will to send scientists to the moon to set up a laboratory and drill down into the core of the moon to investigate this problem. Scientists had to do something that education researchers do all the time—come up with a way to observe the immediately unobservable. Much like we have to come up with some way to conceptualize and theorize what learning "looks like," scientists had to accept that they had to investigate the existence of something beyond simple or direct observation. Their solution was, in my mind, rather brilliant. They decided to smash a projectile into the surface of the moon. In the instant the projectile met the surface of the moon, a plume of debris and "stuff" was released into the thin atmosphere of the moon. The scientists captured this debris—this "stuff"—for the traces of chemicals that would indicate the presence of water on/in the moon. Their access route to investigation was in an immediate outcome of a collision that caused a disturbance in the moon's previous state. The disturbance produced some observable thing that was not really too special (a big cloud of dirt), but what the thing indicated was the significant finding. There is, scientists found, a fair amount of water on the moon. But they didn't collect it in a bucket. They deduced this because of the ways that light refracted through the "plume" that was produced upon impact (Chang, 2009).

Why all of this talk about the moon and water? Instead of asking how to find the water on the moon by shining light through the particles kicked up upon a heavy and fast-moving object slamming violently into the surface, in this chapter I shine the theoretical light of psychoanalysis and difficult knowledge upon the articulations that participants make upon their engagement with representations of social and historical trauma. The psychic phenomena are not immediately observable. One has to look at clues. As I have described, difficult knowledge is a psychic engagement between a person and information that has to do with the suffering, pain, and trauma of others. The concurrent problem as elaborated by Pitt and Britzman (2003) is that difficult knowledge resists articulation and, thus, what is investigated cannot be directly observed by a researcher. The unconscious is not directly knowable. What I am left to do, then, is to investigate the particles that arise from the collision between pedagogical projectiles and the surface of the individual. Here, the projectile is a difficult film, photograph, or even memory that comes to mind through discussion. The "affective plume" (as I call it) that arises from the initial contact is emotion, or affect. In psychoanalytic theory, affects and emotions are the clues, the indicants, the sign posts, which help demonstrate the ways in which people make connections to objects in the world.

A research methodology drawing from such a theoretical perspective is derived from a desire to investigate the interplay between external events and/or representations of them and the internal processes of meaning making. As such, psychoanalysis offers "convincing explanations of how the 'out-there' gets 'in-here' and vice versa, especially through concepts such as projection, internalization and identification" (Frosh, 2003, p. 347). Although perhaps convincing to some, there are serious doubts levied against psychoanalytic approaches to empirical studies arising from the ways that researchers are prone to inappropriate self-positioning as the "one who knows" what is going on within the psyche of the participant. I acknowledge this danger and shortcoming, and I certainly do not pretend to know the psychic lives of the participants.

In attempt to avoid that danger, researchers using psychoanalysis in their present interpretations fully admit to the limits of the investigation. The articulations offered by participants were prompted by my questions. My position as a white male (and their subject positions as described below), their former instructor, and researcher all have considerable consequences for the ways that they spoke about the film (the film itself, is also discussed below). Although I fully acknowledge the ways that these make significant differences, I contend that reading data psychoanalytically can be generative for us in the social studies where issues of race, sexuality, class, war, violence, and politics dominate the curricular terrain and where emotional outcomes are sure to arise.

Aparna Mishra Tarc (2013) warns us that in light of a psychoanalytic and postcolonial understanding of subjectivity, "We can no longer take the other at her word as the truth of an existence. We can no longer take our words for that truth either" (p. 548). Such a caution is crucial to research engagements given the complications present in human relationships, such as those that occur in education and, in particular, in social studies education. What it means is that what any individual says does not convey any sort of transparent or self-evident meaning. Words are in need of interpretation, and indeed, those interpretations are undertaken by people with an overpopulated set of intentions as well. Tarc continues with a pedagogical and methodological suggestion that "traces of affective material left behind in writing provide us with the resources to unravel carefully constructed positions on the right or best way to live" (p. 548).

What I seek to do with the data generated through interviews about a particular film is to take a small number of exchanges uttered by social studies teachers and make interpretations about how, or if, a situation of difficult knowledge emerges and, if so, how difficult knowledge circulates in such a setting.

Participants

The individuals who participated in this study were enrolled in a secondary social studies education program at a large Midwestern university during the 2008–2009 school year. These five individuals, two of whom are male (George and Ben), the other four female (Eva, Lynn, Grace, and Patty), are white and middle to upper-middle class. Lynn and Patty were in the midst of their preparation for a year-long student teaching experience. George, Ben, Grace, and Eva had recently completed their certification when I invited them to participate in the study. All of the participants were invited to be part of the study based on their in-class contributions that I had the opportunity to observe either as part of the larger study (Lynn and Patty), or in the role of their methods course instructor (George, Ben, Grace, and Eva). These invitations were not made with the intent of creating some representative sample of students (though they, in many ways, are representative). Rather, I invited these particular students because of their willingness to engage thoughtfully and rather critically in issues of social education. By this I mean that they were eager to discuss issues of race, class, power, and representation and felt that they were important pedagogical stakes in such a consideration. The methodology was predicated upon participants' willingness to talk and think about difficult subject matter. The study was presented to them because of my interest in the ways that social studies teachers respond to and engage with topics involving social and historical trauma.

Research Context

Methods

I distributed copies of the film to the participants in the Spring of 2009 and asked them to watch the film on their own (the film is four hours long, to watch as a group seemed to me a bit impractical), to note their reactions, and to be prepared to talk about their reactions in individual interview settings.

The five participants in the study were all graduates of the teacher education program where the study was conducted and were provided a copy of the film, which they agreed to view on their own time. Active Interviews (Holstein & Gubrium, 1995) were conducted with each of the participants after they viewed this documentary. In this view of interviewing, the researcher and the participants are considered to be subjects who collectively and collaboratively mediate, rather than possess, knowledge. Notes participants took while viewing the film, together with a process of "think aloud" to explore participants' thinking as we viewed particular segments of the film they chose to discuss, were used to guide the interviews. Interviews lasted between forty-five minutes and an hour and took place in a conference room on the campus of the university that housed the study. To begin each interview, I asked each participant to explain what they thought the film was about by prompting them to talk about it as though I were a stranger in a movie store who was asking what the film was about. I asked to them show the clips that they had identified in their notes as those they wished to discuss during our interview. All but one of the participants either did not take notes or did not bring them, so in our conversations we were constantly scrolling through the film itself, stopping when participants remembered something and were prompted to make a comment. When this would happen, I would ask questions about why they thought that section was significant and proceeded to mine their answers from there.

What I hoped to find out is whether or how their reactions to the film varied, the degree to which they were engaged emotionally in it, and whether and how they implicated themselves, social studies issues, and their teaching. After all, "What educates is not the person but the emotional experience of relating that becomes the basis for further meaning" (Britzman, 2006, p. 166). In light of these emotional ways of relating that provide the groundwork for further meaning, and—I think—further teaching, I wanted to know whether and/or how the invitations to knowledge presented in the film were taken up, which were accepted and which were rejected, and how they were discussed.

Further, what I present as data, the words of research participants and my interactions with them, is often not surprising or "new" as far as the content goes. We will see that White teachers, as has been well documented, prefer to avoid directly engaging with issues of race, and participants will work to "protect" the self from being implicated in broad social problems. Instead of presenting what might seem to be novel articulations or actions (they are not), I present what I find in another way—one not present within the social studies literature—of interpreting those actions; the focus is on the "how" rather than the "what."

Lacan suggests that in psychoanalysis spoken language (speech) is given "back its dignity, so that it does not always represent for them those words, devalued in advance, that force them to fix their gaze elsewhere" (Lacan, 1998, p. 18). We are asked to think not about the act of speaking itself (not just the intended meaning), but the difference that act, or knowledge, or statement makes (Felman, 1982). Giving speech back its dignity means that speech is doing more than communicating discrete facts, and that giving value to speech begins with the presumption that what we say carries with it a desire to communicate something else, something else that might be outside of conscious awareness. We say more than we know.

Routing and Re-Routing of Difficult Knowledge

The pedagogical invitation offered to elicit these processes was a viewing and discussion of *When the Levees Broke—A Requiem in Four Acts*, a documentary film that confronts the impact Hurricane Katrina had on the people of New Orleans. Directed by Spike Lee and presented in two parts on back-to-back nights on HBO in 2006, the film is provocative in its portrayal of the victims and also the manner in which the "natural" disaster (the hurricane itself) gives way to a human crisis underwritten by human error. It is, in essence, a film in which the viewer is confronted with a disturbing picture of race and class relations, the inadequacy of our government's response to crisis, and the inequitable ways in which those elements (government response, class, and race) relate.

The film itself is comprised of news footage shot during the hurricane and its immediate aftermath as well as interviews with those who live, and have lived, in New Orleans.[1] The viewer is asked to confront several tragic stories: A man watches his mother die while waiting for assistance to arrive at the New Orleans Superdome, a husband watches his wife carried away in the flood waters, elderly without medicine, children without clothes, and families without homes. Race, of course, is foregrounded as an issue in the film and is both present and avoided in the discussions the participants and I had about it. New Orleans itself is what we might call an African American city—over 60% of the population of the city is African American—but in the most vulnerable parts of the city the population becomes decreasingly diverse, and in the lower 9th ward (the area most terribly affected in the flooding) the population is 98% African American. Most of the speakers in the film are African American, and a great deal of attention is given to the ways that this group was, and has been, wronged in various situations related to the hurricane as well as by other historical processes in the United States.

Route 1: From Student to Teacher to Student

One of the expectations in teacher education is that teachers should think about their own learning, their teaching, and their students. Students in education programs are asked to write educational autobiographies in order to become aware of their predispositions to schooling and learning. Later, we remind our student-teachers that they are not teaching content, that they are teaching students about content. Learner-centered instruction is put at a premium. Teaching is, in this sense, about the students. And what the participants talk about here—Eva and Ben in this section—has a great deal of focus on their students. But as I will show, moving quickly from "self" to "student," while obviously something we want to have happen, also prevents some other forms of thinking from happening. In this movement from self to other, I wonder, are some things lost? Can that desired result of teacher education also manifest itself as a retreat from certain issues, an avoidance, and a place where the difficulties and complexities that are incurred as a result of learning might be placed upon students rather than dealt with by the teachers?

Psychoanalytic theory lets us investigate such questions. Although I use the language of routing and re-routing, these are processes that involve the ego defense mechanisms. These defenses are the road signs and detours, the strategies by which we avoid the uneven terrain of the construction zone that is being made from the mix of our past experiences and how we variously engage and avoid them. One of the ways that difficult knowledge and the knower gets re-routed, one potential detour, is placing our uncertainties on others. Again, this is something every one of us does, every day, indeed all the time. Instead of tolerating ambiguity and complexity, admitting to ourselves that things might be more or less troubling than we previously imagined, we allow ourselves certainty and (basically) give the complexities to some other. This particular difficulty of difficult knowledge is itself multi-layered, particularly when considered in the context of a student/teacher. The encounter is at once felt to be of consequence for the self and for their students. It is a task of making some kind of sense of the trauma being engaged and then trying to navigate the complex and ambiguous task of making that trauma into pedagogy, into a lesson to be learned by others.

Eva, for example, explains how the film raised a series of questions that she claims to not be able to answer. She wonders how it could be that the structures put in place to protect people failed so miserably in New Orleans in the aftermath of Hurricane Katrina. The re-routing works in the beginning of this exchange through the ways in which Eva avoids answering the questions she poses to herself. She is eventually able to offer answers. To do so, however, she has to imagine answering her students.

> Eva: I ask questions about how something like this could happen and exist without anyone doing anything. And it makes me think: So they should die? Because they can't swim? So I didn't…I just…why to them, why here, and why didn't we fix this?
>
> Jim: Can you answer any of those questions?
>
> Eva: No.
>
> Jim: Maybe not definitely …but how would you answer those questions?
>
> Eva: I picture students coming to me and saying "Ms. Eva, why didn't anyone take care of those people?" And I can't answer that question.
>
> Jim: Really?
>
> Eva: Because they didn't care.
>
> Jim: That's an answer.
>
> Eva: They don't care. They were in Iraq. And Louisiana didn't have what they were concerned about. That's how I feel.

There are plenty of processes at play in this short excerpt from a female student teacher reacting to a difficult documentary film. In the context of this inquiry, however, I would call attention to a pattern of movements in Eva's articulations as she struggles to deal with what she saw in the film and, mostly, with how to address that "seeing" in a pedagogical encounter. Codified in this brief exchange is a situation in which Eva asks a series of cascading questions, ending with her imagination of a response to an imaginary question from imaginary students. More, though, Eva has encountered difficult knowledge—difficult in its very imagery and difficult to address pedagogically—and is unsure how to engage it in the context of the pervading narratives within social studies, ones that, more often than not, portray government as a force in-the-know, one that is responsive to its citizens and treats them equally and fairly.

But as we delve more deeply into this dialogue, more becomes apparent: One may ask, as I do, using the lens of difficult knowledge, why is it that Eva first claims the inability to answer the questions? And when she does give herself permission to answer the questions, in many ways (at this point) superficially, she has to do so when imagining her own students posing the questions. She also implicates herself in the problem in her interrogating why "we" did not do anything to fix the problem or address the issue. Immediately after this she contends that she cannot answer those questions she has posed. She moves from the inclusive "we" to an unnamed "they," removing herself from implication in the process, a first routing away from the self and onto the other.

She also marks a distinction between "knowing" and "feeling," delineating a separation between the affective world of emotion and the desire for stable and certain knowledge. The difficulty here has to do with the way that Eva takes her uncertainty, her initial inability to answer, and re-routes it into the circuitry of the learning encounter that she imagines happening with her students. Something gets in the way of her answering her own questions, perhaps acting to protect some belief or disposition that may lead to discomfort. Her eventual response, that perhaps those in power "care" less about those who do not have valued resources to offer, might provoke some anxiety. After all, this kind of thinking explicitly counters the narratives—the egalitarian and meritocratic ideal—that most commonly circulate about our society. This kind of counter narrative can be troubling, particularly if there are not other narrative structures in which to place the discomfort. It seems here that Eva takes this discomfort and uses the narrative structure of the pedagogical encounter with her students as a location in which to place it.

For example, Eva continues by alluding to a part of the film where several citizens of the lower 9th ward of New Orleans claimed to have heard bombs going off when the levees broke. This section of the film reminds the viewer that in 1927 the local government decided to explode the levees in a particular way so as to flood the areas of town with lower property values; keeping the larger, more expensive homes and families safe. The possibility of this happening has a clear impact on Eva's thinking about society and the ways that different individuals are treated in it. What she says here continues directly from the first exchange.

> When I heard in the section that talked about the flood of '27 and questions about intentional bombing.... Does this happen? If it does, how do I not know about it? If it does, how do people sleep? If it does, does our democracy work? Or do you as a pres-

ident get so far removed from your people that you don't think about these things. And you think of resources instead of lives? So I think I could answer personally how I feel to students, but I don't know if I could...are they the right answers? Is this really what happened?

As with the above example, we see the interaction with this film as inviting a steady stream of questions from Eva. She is posing questions whose answers could potentially open conversations about the nature of our society, the way it works, and the relationships between government and citizens. Those are important topics for social studies teachers. But the questions seem to be imbued with anxiety, and they could even be read rhetorically as indicating Eva's sentiments here—that "this" does happen, that our democracy does not work, and that our government places a higher value on resources than people. It may be that her anxiety is not centered on the fate of the citizens of New Orleans. It may not be about being able to correct an issue or assign blame. Because when Eva asks, "How do I not know about this?" she is giving voice to an anxiety about what are felt as truths (at least suspected truths, she only approaches them through questions) outside of her conscious awareness. Her suspicions are routed into questions to be taken up as issues with which to confront with her students. Far from inappropriate, it is precisely this kind of move that individual pedagogues make on a regular basis. However, it is important to focus on the processes, the backstories, and the motivations behind those questions if we are to understand the pedagogical endeavor in greater detail and complexity.

Eva does experience the possibility of a concrete government policy to destroy life and property as a topic to be debated in a social studies class, but it is experienced as her "feelings," in some ways intended to be off-limits in her pedagogical life. Yet it is clear that in Eva's own learning, the knowledge that makes a difference is felt as emotion, something beyond rational thought. However, if we recall that earlier distinction between "knowing" and "feeling" and the attendant complexities that this distinction raises for her imagined pedagogy, she is not only resisting her own affective knowing, she is also resisting the possibility of uncovering her students' emotional worlds. Such a distinction marks a desire to avoid the kinds of conflict that are instantiated upon the introduction of complexity into classroom life. What about this kind of conflict allows Eva to foreclose such complexity? Further, what are the consequences this pattern of thinking would have on what Eva would and would not engage with her students in her own social studies classroom?

Britzman (2003) notes "students are suspicious of any knowledge that bothers their wishes for certainty and control, even as many also can admit their discomfort at feeling controlled by others and the pleasure that they make from the experience of doubt" (p. 77). When Eva is resistant to answering the very questions she poses to herself, I see evidence of both such a suspicion and a wish for certainty. She seems to be caught in a negotiation between those feelings and a concurrent wish to share those feelings with her students, complete with the ambiguities and pleasures derived from doubt. Yet she is uncertain in her struggles with whether the latter wish could be fulfilled in pedagogy due to an anxiety about what such an act would provoke in the classroom. Put differently, just as she is reluctant to acknowledge the propositions forwarded in the film as truth rather than feeling, she is similarly reluctant to share those kinds of propositions with her students.

Eva is also upset about having information withheld, of being left in a state of ignorance, an experience where the trauma was not just on seeing fellow human beings suffering but feeling a personal threat to her previously stable worldview. And she ends this section by directing the question back to me—the interviewer, her former teacher—and she wonders if there is something wrong with posing particular questions to her students. Such a line of questioning is a further manifestation of moving her complexity someplace else.

For Eva, then, difficult knowledge is routed from self to her students so that it can return to her once again under the guise of mastery ("Can I tell them something if I do not know that it's true?"). In this return, she is able to articulate her feelings in terms of what she would tell (or withhold from) her students.

Although Ben's impressions of the film differ from Eva's, his descriptions of WTLB indicate a similar kind of re-routing that takes the information from the film and direct it quickly into helping "teach a lesson" to others without understanding first what the lesson might be for the self. In our conversation, Ben stated that he did not cry when he watched WTLB and was surprised that he did not. He explained that he was not sure why this was the case and proposed perhaps because he had a cold that his eyes were dry. For whatever reason, Ben's emotions were routed away from those avenues he expected his emotions would run. I wondered about whether his raced and classed position (Ben is an upper-middle-class white male) in society might have had something to do with the lack of emotional connection to the suffering portrayed in the film.

Jim: One thing that I have to ask is: Is it hard to see yourself in that film? Being from where you're from, being who you are, and I don't mean this to be accusing in any way, could that be part of it?

Ben: Maybe I don't see myself in it. That's interesting…maybe that is part of it. That is something I have thought about, not even just in teaching but just talking to people about poverty and oppression, I wonder how I can ever understand that because the only thing I've ever been is a rich white boy. And you know, so is it the same to be able to teach it and not be able to connect to it like that, so maybe that is part of it. And I know that is something that I was thinking about too, that some of the people in the film just seem like caricatures in the way that they act and I just remember wondering if I could take them seriously. So yeah, maybe that's part of it, and that is troublesome. I hadn't really looked at it that way, it's totally possible, I'm not going to say, "oh yeah, that's totally it."

In the statements above I find Ben working through a new idea. He is able to acknowledge that as a self-described "rich white boy" he may be differently equipped to confront issues of poverty and race with his own students. That he is able to voice his reactions in terms of uncertainty and consideration is, I think, quite a sophisticated move for a social studies teacher to be equipped to make. We want our social studies teachers to be able to consider openly the effects of race and class on their (and their students') teaching and learning. Still, there is a significant re-routing happening here. We have an example where Ben moves quickly away from the question I had asked. I asked about seeing himself in the film, and he moved to consider his own students and the lessons that might be learned from watching the film in his class. It is a rapid move from self to other. Ben routes a consideration of the ways his race impacts the way he learned during the encounter with this film and instead discusses the way it impacts his teaching of the content. He is talking about race and class, issues central to what I consider to be a good social studies education, but he is deflecting the conversation away from self, and onto the "other" of his imagined students and how he imagines their interactions with the individuals in the film.

There are reasons to suspect that because I had been Ben's methods instructor that he relied on a discourse appropriate to the context in which we had initiated and, in many senses, rehearsed through two semesters' worth of class meetings. Viewed in this way, his moves to talk about teaching might not seem too surprising. Another way to read this exchange, though, and assuming that speaking subjects are always and already fulfilling many different aims simultaneously, is that the movements from self to other are significant in other ways. Although it stands to reason that Ben, as a social studies teacher, would think about teaching, throughout the above exchange I see evidence of how these different routes might be working through some of his emotional baggage of this engagement with difficult knowledge. Because it is not only that the consideration moves from self to other that bears significance. The very engagement with the knowledge and his own emotions is important also. For example, Ben moves away from the subject of crying and toward counting ("The first time they showed a dead body. I was like, 'you know what? I want to see how many dead bodies they show.' I noticed they show 1, they show a couple more, then they show 25 in a row."). He moves away from that which is felt irrationally and toward what can be tallied and concrete. Ben explains away his emotions in terms of his teaching and his students. He does so, and this is an example of the re-routing of difficult knowledge. It is not always obvious or immediately felt. Instead, the re-routing is often what might be called a compromise, a strategy of dealing with discomfort through the perceived path of least resistance. While discussing topics and issues crucial to social studies education—the critical analysis of text, the ways that class and race impact pedagogical possibility—his talk would seem to be completely "on topic." But the topic taken up in his speech during this interview protects the self in many ways. Although we cannot know what it is exactly Ben is avoiding without further analysis, there is certainly evidence that he moves away from implicating his own ideas and thoughts. Seeing a route taken toward the very important issues of Ben's own race and class but, at the same time, also a re-routing of difficult knowledge to keep him safe from a perceived threat, I asked Ben about his lack of emotional connection to this film.

> I'm surprised to say that it wasn't. And I don't know why. Like…not to be creepy, but I filled out a "movies that made you cry" survey, and I saw that [survey] after I watched it. And I didn't cry, and I'm surprised by that because I cry pretty easily when it comes to that kind of stuff. During my WWII unit we watched, *Pearl Harbor*, *WWII*, and *Band of Brothers*. It was really hard for me, especially the *Band of Brothers* lesson. I was like "This is going to be a tough lesson. You need to get out of this, like you need to be strong for the students." Because when I watched it the night before I got done and just sat for a while, because it really engaged me. And so I was kind of shocked that I didn't get really upset by this because I watch a lot of documentaries and they usually do.

A few issues are worth mentioning. If Ben was not emotionally engaged by this film, that would be absolutely fine. He could have said something like, "You know what, Jim? I was not moved by this film." What takes on signif-

icance here is the degree to which Ben qualifies his lack of emotional connection and this could be because he wants to be a "good" interview subject.
What I choose to focus on, though, is first how he seems to draw a direct tie
to emotional connection with the physical act of crying. I did not ask him (at
this point) whether he cried while watching the film, yet he moves quickly to
his not doing so. Further, and again exemplifying the detour away from the
self, he quickly moves from the particular content of this film to other films
that he uses in his own teaching, films that did, I suppose, move him closer to
the tears that connote (for him) emotional connection. But as he continues
to discuss those films he uses in his own practice, there is an added layer of
prevention on his physical expression of emotions: his students.

The Significance of Placing Uncertainty Onto the Student

What we've heard thus far from Ben and Eva are not refusals, nor confrontations with the teacher or researcher, they are strategies that re-route discourse
away from the traumatic but are still within the confines of the investigation.
In their movement from self to other, Ben and Eva remove the ambiguity of
feelings and emotions from themselves in exchange for considering ambiguities in terms of their students.

As I have written repeatedly, social studies education is often the stuff
of difficult knowledge. At the same time, though, social studies curriculum
asks students to undertake all sorts of conversations that, while pedagogically
sound and educationally appropriate, help to avoid the difficulties of difficult
knowledge and the concurrent confronting of our ultimate vulnerabilities and
our uncertainties with the world. Mock trials about the teaching of evolution,
debates about abortion and the death penalty, structured academic controversy about the dropping of the atomic bomb—each of these, more often than
not, takes a route away from thinking about the actuality of these events. By
focusing on whether the atomic bomb should have been dropped, for example, we often avoid the consideration of what happened to the hundreds of
thousands of people on whom the bomb was (despite whatever structured
arguments are made about it in a classroom) dropped. This kind of re-routing
carries with it an attractive logic: We can take the traumas of the past and,
through rational debate and procedure, prevent future ones from taking place.
There is no doubt that rational debate and democratic procedure through
policy issues are important skills for students to cultivate. I am hoping to highlight what else those activities do, and in some sense that can, it seems, steer

the learner away from the actuality of death and suffering that are part of the historical record.

That is, whether or not we acknowledge the traumas of the past as such, they are there, and more often than not are avoided. They are taken up within other, more readily available discourses. As I demonstrated above, Ben and Eva take what I consider to be their own discomfort and re-route it into the discourse of their students. It is a release valve for difficult knowledge.

The issues of avoidance and resistance take on a different order for a social studies teacher who does, in fact, confront these issues in a more direct manner. These kinds of teachers are asking their students to do something that is somewhat unnatural, "to confront perspectives, situations, and ideas that may not be just unfamiliar but appear at first glance as a criticism of the learner's view" (Britzman, 1998, p. 11). In other words, in considering multiple perspectives, particularly as they relate to the issues of race, class, and systemic violence, the student may feel as though their own perspective is flawed. The implications, then, become the greatest for those social studies teachers who—if I may—teach the way we want them to teach.

Route 2: From Race to Class

One of the things about difficult knowledge is that the lessons do not fit nicely into what we already know about the world. And when things do not fit we have to find some place for them. Sometimes the knowledge gets rejected ("That can't be; I don't believe that"), sometimes it is accommodated, and as we see with Eva and Ben it is siphoned away and rerouted. In the example here, the routing went to others. Here, as I will show, the routing is in relationship to a social world, but it is at the same time a relationship to a particular way of knowing. Alcorn (2013) writes of the desire not to know as a process where first:

> There is movement toward knowing. There is an emergent knowledge working itself toward consciousness. This transfer of knowledge takes place not from one person to another person, but from one sector of the self that desires to know to a different sector of the self that desires not to know. (p. 49)

What Alcorn identifies is what I see occurring in the encounter with the difficult knowledge of race by many white social studies teachers. This is not a new area of study. Several education researchers have taken up the idea that race is an issue of consequence for social studies education (see, for example,

Epstein, 1998) as well as something that is avoided and circumvented in similar ways to those I will describe below.

For example, Dickar (2000) deploys a Foucauldian understanding of discourse to aid in the understanding of how race continues to remain an oppressive force in education. Although she does not couch her findings in terms of psychoanalytic theory, there are certainly overlapping interests in that she explores the ways that race is "deflected," "evaded," and placed into individualistic discourses. Similarly, Haviland (2008) categorizes the ways that race talk is avoided within a critical discourse analysis focused on illustrating how race and power interrelate and overlap. She finds that white teachers avoid race by using several strategies, including "avoiding words, false starts, letting others off the hook, and changing the subject" (p. 44). My consideration here corroborates the findings of these studies but offers a focus not on the fact that race is avoided, but instead on the processes involved in such avoidance.

Of the issues, scenes, and emotions that the participants shared with me in our conversations, there was one common denominator: Each of them made at least a passing reference to Kanye West and his appearance in the film. Let us remember that Kanye's Hurricane Katrina moment came during a national telethon when he went off-script (this before "going Rogue" was en vogue) and said, "George Bush does not care about black people," while standing beside a shocked and speechless Mike Myers.

When the Levees Broke is nearly four hours in length and filled with testimony from citizens famous and anonymous. That Kanye West makes unprovoked appearances in the participants' reactions, then, is noteworthy. It begs several questions. First, what is the degree to which our popular culture informs what we find important or worthy of comment? Some of the participants, like Ben for example, found it odd that West appeared in the film at all. His concern was whether all celebrities should get equal treatment or if West was showcased or highlighted for some reason. Patty, who sympathized with West, was concerned with how we were not privy to the rest of West's comments. West makes a most provocative statement about race. In the United States the topic of race and its history is constituted of a set of difficult knowledge unto itself. Forced migrations, servitude in slavery, the injustice of Jim Crow, public lynchings, and the tragedy of Hurricane Katrina serve as reminders that despite our election of an African American president, the issue of race is far from settled. In these interviews, though, the topic of race is re-routed toward the issues of class.

West's statement was heavily treated in the popular media. West's statement directly and explicitly invokes the notion of race being of the utmost importance to the conversation about the aftermath of Katrina, and while all of the participants commented on his appearance in the film, they also avoided discussing race. In order to begin to illustrate this rerouting, I borrow from my discussion with Lynn. I asked her what she found interesting about the clip she chose to discuss with me.

> Lynn: Well I just think it's really interesting that like, Kanye says "George Bush does not care about black people," they show the clip, and then they show three people who are automatically like, "Well he's saying this because we have to see where he's coming from, he was just trying to speak from the heart." These sound like excuses to me. And for Al Sharpton to say that he was saying something constructive. Like how is that constructive? In juxtaposition to that, when Bush is clearly speaking without a script, without a teleprompter, and he tells Michael Brown he's doing a great job, we don't hear, there's nobody on the right…or nobody to defend Bush coming in after playing that video clip and saying, "Well he meant this, or he is speaking off camera, or he was trying to relate to the people." You don't have any of that.

Lynn is concerned about the treatment Kanye West received in the film. She seems frustrated and upset that there was not a voice that represented the idea that George Bush did and does, in fact, care about black people. I take Lynn to understand Kanye West's statements as a mistake, something that needed to be corrected or apologized for. Perhaps because of this, she seems to view the subsequent speakers in the film (all praising West's statements) as apologizing for Kanye West. Lynn is equating what she perceives as West's misstatements with Bush's comment that has been played and replayed in which he commends then director of FEMA, Michael Brown.

Each of these might be fair interpretations of these scenes in the film. What she does not do, though, is take up the issue that was explicitly addressed by West, that of the treatment of African Americans in New Orleans following this hurricane. This is not my concern here. What I am choosing to focus on is the immediate move away from the issue of race. The topic of race is rerouted into a discussion about how West's statement was destructive. I asked her why this was the case. She responded by saying:

> Clearly people are already angry in this situation. So all he is doing is polarizing people, which he said it did, there was definitely a tension in the room. And it's not solving a problem, it's just complaining about it. If you think George Bush doesn't like black people, then whatever. But is that really the platform that you should be

using when people are suffering? Whites and Blacks? I think that turns it into a race thing. It turns it into a race thing.

In Lynn's elaboration she is laying claim to a position that race should not be an issue that is used divisively. If focus is placed upon race, she seems to be saying, there is more—not less—trouble. I use this exchange to highlight the ways that Lynn moves around race, first toward but then away from it. I then asked to her consider Kanye West's statements as a perspective worthy of taking seriously. She notes the anger that was being exhibited throughout the film, but race seems to be off limits as part of the equation of this anger. I wondered, then, how this anger should have been expressed. Lynn replied,

> I guess he could make it more of a general statement. Like the government doesn't seem to care about us. Or, the government is acting ineptly and people are dying because of their mistakes. I think that would have been a valid point of view.

Notice that Lynn's recommendation for how to make a more constructive argument is to remove race altogether. Race is made silent; it is removed from the statement. More than this, though, any reference to an individual is taken out of this statement as well. Rather than mention George Bush, Lynn would prefer Kanye West to have implicated "the government." Instead of talking about black people, West should have simply used an inclusive pronoun. While acknowledging that people are losing their lives in the process, Lynn takes the individual, and their race, out of the equation.

Where Lynn is angered by the ways that race is taken up and would rather it be absent from the conversation about the aftermath of Hurricane Katrina, Patty reroutes race in a way that places it into a context of class and unrestrained capitalism. She uses Kanye West's statements as a way to allude to race without really investing in this as an issue. First, Patty responds to a question of how she personally felt in response to West's statements. Earlier in our interview she described the movie as being about the way that race played a crucial factor in the government response to the situation in New Orleans and that statement serves as the departing point for this exchange.

> Patty: I feel lucky I guess. I mean just I think it's in the last act where one of the guys that's wearing tinted glasses brings his mom back to her house and she just breaks down. And it's like, I'm never going to have to know what that feels like. I don't live in a place where that would happen and I'm the right class and race for all of that.

Jim: It's interesting because you described the movie about race. In many ways it is. If you or I were African American, would you describe the movie differently?

Patty: Maybe. But I think it was just as much about class as it was about a race. But I think that if I were talking to a black person that I would include a comment about race. There's an awful lot of pissed-off black people in this, and I agree with them to some extent.

Jim: But not all the way?

Patty: I mean, there were an awful lot of white people who lost everything too. And so I hesitate to say it's just a race issue when you've got the woman who just has a tent on the foundation of her house, ya know. And it's I think that New Orleans is a diverse enough city that it was poor people of every race that were affected.

Jim: Definitely.

Patty: But I also don't like making things about race. I don't know. I hate to say that it's just race, because I feel like there's more to it.

Patty is obviously correct that the problems in New Orleans were not just simply about race. But what is interesting here is not Patty's ability to parse social problems into their constituent parts, although it is certainly important for social studies educators to be able to do so. Instead, it is in her disposition to avoid the particular aspects of the situation that do have to do with race.

According to the US Census Bureau, African Americans account for 67% of the population of New Orleans. Further, according to data published by the GNO Community Data Center, African Americans account for 98% of the population of the Lower Ninth Ward, the area that was most heavily affected by the breach of the levees (http://www.gnocdc.org/orleans/8/22/people.html). So although Patty is correct that there were plenty of white people who were affected by the flooding, African Americans were disproportionally represented in the areas where the consequences of the broken levees were direst. Had I presented her with these data, she may have reconsidered her views. The point here, though, and Patty even articulates this desire, is that she has a preference for not "making things about race." She also admits to her race contributing to her perception that a situation like this would never happen to her. So it is not the case that Patty has a conceptual framework that prevents her from seeing her whiteness as a privilege. Despite this acknowledgment, and perhaps because of this privilege, she is able to not make things about race in ways that she might revise in the company of an African American person. In other words, she seems to avoid race as a compelling issue to take on as a singular topic because she can.

Maybe what is occurring here has something to do with an inability to distinguish between the experiences of others and the experiences of the self. Or, as Britzman (2003) offers, "Something difficult occurs in helping relationships. We are apt to forget our differences" (p. 6). When we enter into a relationship in which our conscious motivation is to educate, our tendency is to think of the other as we think of ourselves. It is common in methods classes to hear students/teachers talk about the creation of an activity or lesson that they remember being significant and successful in their own learning. These activities similarly ignore the differences between self and other and preclude the teacher from being able to consider the individuals under his or her care as having their own situations, desires, and histories. This might help explain why these white, relatively affluent, individuals can easily (or so it seems) avoid discussing race. Grace articulates

> Hurricane Katrina was Kanye West going on TV and saying that George Bush hates black people and that's how it was portrayed and that's how people remember it: You know the terrible conditions that black people were living in this country. And I never really understood the racial aspect of it; I just thought it was more of a class thing. So I've been sort of resistant to the idea that this is the shining example of race in America. Yes, we've got this underlayer of society that we are not caring for, but that is more so about greed and unrestrained capitalism I would say.

As was the case with Patty, Grace attributes the problems of New Orleans to unrestrained capitalism. She acknowledges West's assertion about race and then immediately moves away from race and toward class. These statements, while avoiding race, still are important indicators that these future social studies teachers are considering these issues as interrelated and perpetuating social inequity. Still, it is curious that although class can be taken as a singular issue, race, for these participants, cannot. Part of this, of course, is based on the well-trodden terrain of white privilege, but part of white privilege is an avoidance of understanding the white self as raced and, vis-à-vis this particular race, positioned in advantageous ways.

The Significance of Routing Away from Race

There are many ways to discuss Hurricane Katrina, yet all of the participants chose to focus, at least for a moment, on the scene with Kanye West. Why is that? In what way does this focused attention operate? I find that this focus is a way to route themselves away from Hurricane Katrina. After all, Kanye West was talking about race, and did so during a telethon to raise money for the survivors of the flood. In a way, what the participants are doing is talking about someone else talking about Hurricane Katrina and the way they felt it highlighted an ongoing racial issue in the United States. It is not only a route away from race, but also a route away from talking about the specificity of Katrina. It is a movement away from discussing Katrina and its aftermath to a discussion of talk about it. The signifier (the talk) becomes the signified (that which took place), and, in the process that which is signified (Katrina) takes a back seat to its representation. It becomes a form of discourse about discourse rather than a discourse about the event the discourse is attempting to describe—a way of avoiding the discussion about Katrina through a privileging of a comment about a response (or lack thereof) to it.

These are students who have taken courses that specifically address race and privilege and whose methods courses asked them to confront similar issues through the works of authors like hooks (1994), Ladson-Billings (1995), Villegas and Lucas (2002), and Epstein (1998). Despite all of this work, the participants here avoid race for various reasons that cannot be explained in any certain terms. And the reasoning is not the issue of import here. Instead, the issue is simply in noting the patterns, the fact that routing and re-routing occur based in some kind of psychic formula designed to protect the self from the kinds of discomfort that are anxiety provoking in that they reveal the self to be in some way implicated in the suffering, pain, and loss of others.

In this sense, then, this section does not reveal new issues. It is not a novel observation that white people have difficulty understanding race and its effects in pedagogy (see the entire body of research on culturally relevant pedagogy). What it does, though, is attempt to pry open the lid that contains and obscures the processes behind such avoidances and resistances (Garrett & Segall, 2013; Segall & Garrett, 2013). What I mean here, couched more psychoanalytically, is that Grace and Patty get close to race, even mention it specifically, before quickly reorienting the conversation to other issues, and therefore this is evidence of the instantiation of some mechanism of defense, those mechanisms that act as the re-routers of difficult knowledge.

Race matters in social studies education. To think about race in the classroom, though, means being able to talk about it openly and honestly. The re-routing that takes place here indicates to me that further work must be done in various pedagogical locations to help white teachers engage with race as a singular issue. The significance of this re-routing lies in the ways we can note that certain topics are treated with more or less comfort in their practice. After all, if these participants are rerouting their thoughts away from race onto other political and social issues in these interviews, I conclude that similar things will happen in their classrooms.

Conclusions

The stories told in this chapter, and the analysis offered, are undertaken to explore the scene of difficult knowledge in social studies education. In this setting the focus is on teachers who are positioned, somewhat at least, as students. That is, as a researcher and their former course instructor I had the position of initiating the inquiry, choosing the text, asking the questions, and making the interpretations. The analogue to the classroom would have me as the teacher and the participants as the students. The social studies teachers are asked to comment on their reactions to a viewing of a film that represents a great deal of social studies content, both in the formal sense of disciplinary knowledge (history, geography, etc.) and in the more critical sense of calling attention to issues of equity, race, and injustice. The participants are implicated in the events of film as citizens, as they ostensibly carry the responsibility to elect the representatives who craft and enforce the policies that would underwrite the conditions making such social devastation possible.

Methodologically, the concept of routing aids in a visualization of how knowledge is on the move and therefore orients the nature of interpretation of the nature of how people talk through their reactions to a film. Of course, the example above does not convey "the" story. There are many ways that the data presented here could be understood. In fact there are many "correct" interpretations of the data. The point of this chapter is not to tell "the" story of social studies teachers watching an emotionally and politically charged documentary but to ask questions about what kinds of understanding we can come to while thinking about "one" version of the story. The version of the story here focuses on the emotional terrain of such encounters—encounters that force us to confront the most terrifying aspects of the human condition: the death of family, loss, powerlessness, and inequity.

I contend that if we are to concern ourselves with the way that trauma can be "sweetened for easy ingestion, stripped of its horror, impotency, grandeur, and contingency" as Schweber (2006, p. 30) found in her study of Holocaust pedagogy, we would benefit from a kind of thinking about trauma that holds such a sweetening as a defense against a knowing, a routing away from discomfort, and influenced by the ease with which such a curriculum can be manifested within our dominant frameworks of thinking.

Those who are concerned with work that might be termed "social justice" or "critical" want our social studies teachers to confront those issues that are "critical," we want them to introduce to students issues of injustice and inequity so as to bring them to awareness. I think this is what WTLB does/did for the participants of this study. The problem, though, is that there are consequences to this kind of pedagogy. The consequences are neither meant to be warnings against nor reasons to avoid, but they are important. In other words, what if we get what we want? What happens when students in our teacher education programs "do" the things we want them to "do"? Then what (Garrett & Segall, 2015)? How might students be taught that social studies education is a place where, instead of a singular narrative of world history is proffered as preparation, our ties to the world are examined and discussed as more complicated versions of society are encountered and understood.

What I argue for here is an awareness of the features and tendencies of the way we direct our energy, not to lay blame or identify weakness in a pedagogy or methodology but instead to enrich our understanding of the pedagogical situation generally. The notion that individuals re-route is in no way an accusation, a pathologizing, or something that can be overcome. We are all, always, and forever, going to be going toward and away from different frames of awareness. Knowledge is always on the move. The point is that we should be paying attention to such processes so that we can understand what sense students are making from their encounters with difficult knowledge in nuanced, complex ways so that we might be able to equip ourselves (and our student teachers) with as large an arsenal as possible when dealing with the variety and vagary of student reaction to social knowledge. It is crucial that social studies teachers be able to open, rather than foreclose, possibilities for complexity.

Similarly, it is this kind of capacity for empathy and identification that underwrites a consciously acting individual to be a "citizen" who acts in a way that resists injustice and inequity. Perhaps the personal accentuates what is already social inside of us. Possibly it is the other way around. Or maybe the dyadic separation between the two is antiquated by the time anything of significance happens anyway.

Note

1. Social studies educators at Teachers College constructed and freely distributed curricular materials that correspond with the film. See www.teachingthelevees.org for the curriculum itself.

References

Alcorn, M. W. (2013). *Resistance to learning: Overcoming the desire-not-to-know in classroom teaching*. New York, NY: Palgrave Macmillan.

Britzman, D. P. (1998). *Lost subjects, contested objects: Toward a psychoanalytic inquiry of learning*. Albany, NY: SUNY Press.

Britzman, D. P. (2003). *After-education: Anna Freud, Melanie Klein, and psychoanalytic histories of learning*. Albany, NY: SUNY Press.

Britzman, D. P. (2006). *Novel education: Psychoanalytic studies of learning and not learning*. New York, NY: Peter Lang.

Chang, K. (2009, November 14). Water found on moon, researchers say. *The New York Times*. Retrieved from www.nytimes.com

Dickar, M. (2000). Teaching in our underwear: The liabilities of whiteness in the multiracial classroom. In S. Steiner, H. Krank, R. Bahruth, and P. McLaren (Eds.) *Freirean pedagogy, praxis and possibilities: Projects for the new millennium*. (pp. 168–184). New York, NY: Falmer Press.

Epstein, T. (1998). Deconstructing differences in African-American and European-American adolescents' perspectives on US history. *Curriculum Inquiry, 28*(4), 397–423.

Felman, S. (1982). Psychoanalysis and education: Teaching terminable and interminable. *Yale French Studies* (63), 21–44.

Freud, A. (1935/1979). *Psychoanalysis for teachers and parents*. Trans. B. Low. New York, NY: W.W. Norton & Company.

Frosh, S. (2003). *Key concepts in psychoanalysis*. New York, NY: New York University Press.

Garrett, H. J., & Segall, A. (2013). (Re) considerations of ignorance and resistance in teacher education. *Journal of Teacher Education, 64*(4), 294–304.

Garrett, H.J., & Segall, A. (2015). Critical race theory, psychoanalysis, & social studies pedagogy. In P. Chandler (Ed.), *Doing Race in Social Studies: Critical Perspectives*, Charlotte, NC: Information Age Publishing. pp. 279–296.

Haviland, V. S. (2008). "Things get glossed over": Rearticulating the silencing power of whiteness in education. *Journal of Teacher Education, 59*(1), 40–54.

Holstein, J. A., & Gubrium, J. F. (1995). *The active interview* (Vol. 37). Thousand Oaks, CA Sage.

hooks, b. (1994). *Teaching to transgress*. New York, NY: Routledge.

Lacan, J. (1998). The four fundamental concepts of psychoanalysis: The seminars of Jacques Lacan: Book XI. Ed. Jacques-Alain Miller. Trans. Alan Sheridan. New York: W.W. Norton & Company.

Ladson-Billings, G. (1995). Toward a theory of culturally relevant pedagogy. *American Educational Research Journal, 32*(3), 465–491.

Lee, S. (Writer). (2006). *When the Levees Broke: A Requiem in Four Acts*. HBO Video.

Pitt, A., & Britzman, D. (2003). Speculations on qualities of difficult knowledge in teaching and learning: An experiment in psychoanalytic research. *Qualitative Studies in Education, 16*(6), 755–776.

Rankine, C. (2015). *Citizen: An American Lyric*. London: Penguin UK.

Schweber, S. (2006). "Breaking down barriers" or "building strong Christians": Two treatments of Holocaust history. *Theory & Research in Social Education, 34*(1), 9–33.

Segall, A., & Garrett, H.J. (2013). White teachers talking race. *Teaching Education, 24*(3), 265–291.

Tarc, A. M. (2013). Wild reading: this madness to our method. *International Journal of Qualitative Studies in Education, 26*(5), 537–552.

Villegas, A. M., & Lucas, T. (2002). Preparing culturally responsive teachers: Rethinking the curriculum. *Journal of Teacher Education, 53*(1), 20–32.

· 5 ·

THE PRESENCE OF HISTORY AND LEARNING TO TEACH

Novel Reading in Social Studies Education

Despite new thoughts, ideas, and perspectives often being felt as an imposition rather than a revelation, tolerating new ideas or ways of knowing is an integral function in the process of learning. Although what most popularly counts as pedagogy in the public imaginary involves a one-to-one exchange of discrete bits of knowledge that are quantifiable and located within a structure of added value. What is less visible in the public conversations are moments of learning that help students in the process of becoming more creative and healthy individuals situated within healthy and creative communities. And, while the pressures of quantification and value added measures continue to present themselves in all formal educational quarters, the question of how to think of pedagogical work in alternative ways, ways that move toward that transformational moment, remains an open one.

This chapter is concerned with exploring the degree to which breakdown in meaning can lead to new meanings, ones that reach beyond those that would fit nicely into regimes of categorization, ones that can escape the bindings of funding and testing and quantifying. As such, it is offered as part literary critique, case study, and theoretical consideration of pedagogy. I bring those considerations together as a composition representing and demonstrating my investments in both pedagogy and its theorizing. This chapter is not entirely an empirical project, though I use examples from my practice as a teacher educator working with social studies teachers to illustrate possible ways that Toni Morrison's (1987) novel *Beloved* can illustrate the ways in which knowledge is re-formed or re-cognized in the pedagogical scene. I also use data from an uncompleted study about its uses more generally. I focus on what I think reading *Beloved* within a course devoted to pedagogical methods highlights and foregrounds in my own thinking about pedagogy and/in teacher education, and in so doing draw intermittently from students' writing about the book in order to aid in illustrating that thinking. The purpose of the essay is to explore and deliberate on difficult knowledge in social studies teacher education and the scenes of pedagogy more broadly.

To begin, I describe the context in which I assigned Toni Morrison's *Beloved* with a group of pre-service social studies teachers. I then attempt to extend Deborah Britzman's (1998) notion of difficult knowledge by turning to psychoanalyst Jacques Lacan's (2006) notion of "full speech." "Full speech" is a term Lacan used to describe the conditions through which psychoanalytic treatment comes to have effect and, for that reason, is useful for my thinking about the relationship between teaching and learning. Additionally, "full speech" implicates changing structures of knowledge that reorganize events of the past in order to structure future action. In this way it not only relates to pedagogy but also to the relationship between difficult or traumatic history and how those encountering such a history may be enlivened to reconsider particularly impactful modes of relating to the world.

After putting Lacan and Britzman in conversation with one another to extend my understanding of difficult knowledge, I provide an interpretation of what *Beloved* has come to mean to me as a pedagogical text in a teacher education course, including an elaboration of some of the component features of revising old thoughts (recognition) through encounters with difficult narratives in literature.

Difficult knowledge is enmeshed in a pedagogical fabric, from the politics of memorialization to the confounding problem of what counts as a history lesson to the crisis of representation more broadly. But while difficult knowledge is situated within the economy of learning about massive social breakdown and devastation, the difficulty resides not in the content but rather in the learner's relationship with it. The difficulty of difficult knowledge is not only in the horrifying representations of violence imbedded within the study of traumatic histories as they exist in various curricular spaces, but in the ways in which the learners are returned to primal scenes of helplessness and disillusionment vis-à-vis that encounter as they try to make sense of it (Farley, 2009).

As Simon (2014) explains, the difficulty of difficult knowledge

> does not lie inherently within particular artifacts, images, and discourses, or within the histories of those events to which these indexically refer. Rather, the experience of difficulty resides in the problematic but poetic relation between the affects provoked by engaging aspects of the mis-en-scene of an exhibition and the sense articulated within one's experience of this exhibit. (p. 12)

What Simon forwards here is that the status of the learner or viewer's affect is as much under consideration as the formal content of the representation, curriculum text, or artifact that prompts it. There is a type of pedagogical movement that is made possible through the situations of, and in, difficult knowledge.

An imbedded feature within difficult knowledge indicates that there is a type of "learning that proceeds through breakdowns and reparations" where "it is often difficult to decide their differences" (Britzman, 2012, p. 282). The pedagogue, the subject who organizes something of the learning situation, is tasked with the call to intervene in the learners' takenfor-granted notions, their expectations and the degree to which they are laced with psychic investment, and that could very well lead to breakdown. What is more, such an intervention is not always felt to be welcome, pleasant, liberatory, or transformative and indeed may provoke tension, frustration, and anxiety. Knowledge may be experienced as unwelcome.

Therefore, difficult knowledge inaugurates a pedagogical intervention, although one of a different register than the value added quantification of pedagogy that holds sway in the broader public. It can, for example, manifest itself in the white student learning about the history of racism in the US. It can also explode onto the pedagogical scene when learning about structures maintaining injustice and violence; particularly when the learner is for the first time implicating him or herself in those same systems.

The literature on difficult knowledge takes great care in relating the pedagogical present to the traumatic past and delineates the terms of that tense relationship, as I discussed in chapter 2. Matthews (2009) states this problem in terms of an opening. "Instead of closure," she writes, "an encounter with social devastation and loss might bring the self into contact with the reality of one's emotional ties to others" (p. 51). Where the prevailing pedagogical intent in social studies is for students to learn about a particular historical event in sophisticated and disciplined ways, difficult knowledge means that those emotional ties "must be symbolized if the learner is to construct meaning from the meeting of outer and inner world" (p. 51). Simon (2011, 2014) puts this tension not in terms of outer and inner worlds but in terms of affect. His formulation of the potential arising from encounters with difficult knowledge is that they might provide a "shock to thought" through the provision of an affective force, where affect "is a reference to a nonspecific, immediate sensation not pre-coded by a representational system that settles its substance within specific linguistic markers that offer an understanding of just what it is that one is feeling" (p. 11). Simon's move toward affect in relationship to difficult knowledge recognizes that feelings occur before thought.

Difficult Knowledge and Full Speech

What I have come to understand about difficult knowledge is extended by the Lacanian notion of "full speech." I turn to this Lacanian concept here because of the ways it adds an account of possible futures to the conversation of difficult knowledge. Full speech "reorders past contingencies by conferring in them the sense of *necessities to come*, such as they are constituted by the scant freedom through which the subject makes them present" (Lacan, 2006, p. 213, emphasis mine). In other words, the learner is confronting a particular thought or object in the present in which prior ways of knowing are revised for the purposes of some kind of future use. It kicks the footing from beneath the ladder of knowledge or the linear progression of development. Full speech is analyzed not in terms of the content of what is communicated but in terms of what "difference this knowledge makes" (Felman, 1987, p. 56). Lacan acknowledges that full speech is not a feature of everyday life but rather a phenomenon that results from a particular kind of intervention into the empty speech of the patient (2006, p. 208). It is an ideational exchange that makes a demand. The analyst must wait through, must listen, but not act upon, the "empty speech"—that which communicates nothing other than regimented ways of knowing—of the analysand and then offer an intervention that helps the analysand see his or her world from a different vantage point. It allows for new and forward thinking, rather than recursive or past-looking thought.

Difficult knowledge invites and may even produce the kind of knowledge that can lead to the breakdown of our ideas about what will be safe, what will be certain, and what will be open for new ways of knowing (Britzman, 2000). In this sense it has the same kind of forward-looking feature as carried in the notion of "full speech." As such, "difficult knowledge" is a condition, a function of a particular kind of pedagogical intervention, and is comprised of a particular relationship to knowledge. Lacan's "full speech," as I understand its relation to difficult knowledge, is another way to conceptualize the creative and productive potentialities imbedded within this tumultuous process. But what could be productive about such potentially painful confrontations with knowledge?

Such a confrontation can be considered potentially generative because "knowledge is worth just as much as it costs, a pretty penny, in that it takes elbow grease and that it's difficult" (Lacan, 1999, p. 97). The crux of the problem with seemingly new and significant knowledge is that "the difficulty of its exercise is the very thing that is increasing the difficulty of its acquisition" (p. 97). What this means is that a facet of the difficulty of difficult knowledge is in trying to come to grips with its exercise, or to put it more colloquially, its use value. What I mean here is that students in my experience will frequently ask, "what are we supposed to do?" about the particular issue being confronted. This is an exceedingly difficult question in which there is often little that can be done. It means that part of the difficulty of difficult knowledge is settling into that which is disquieting. It may also mean that the more difficult an idea is to conceptualize as being able to immediately deploy in the world, the more difficult that idea is to conceptualize at all. Because of this, it becomes all the more easy to dismiss that not-yet-considered thing as a toss-away, as "bad" knowledge, not relevant, or useless, and becomes folded in the wrinkled relations of ignorance and knowledge (Felman, 1987).

Similarly Britzman (2000) warns that "knowledge use is strictly defined by its capacity to be externalized and applied to others" (p. 204). In order to counter that view of knowledge, she continues, we must find ways of "turning habituated knowledge back on itself and examine its most unflattering features" (p. 204). Turning to the familiar site of social studies education curriculum and standards documents that stand in as the explicit curriculum, this would mean for example thinking about the distance between the narratives of American exceptionalism and the realities of historical transgressions such as slavery, Native American removal, and anti-democratic interventions abroad. But it would not just be thinking about that distance, difficult knowledge also centers the consequence of that consideration and how it would come to have meaning for a particular learner, how that idea would be considered, deliberated, accommodated or resisted. In other words, difficult knowledge is going to center relational modalities occurring in the present that is in relationship to some past.

Context of Inquiry

One of the things I have had problems with as a social studies methods instructor is running up against the limits of what direct instruction can do. I run up against the acknowledgment that I cannot have any direct influence on what a pre-service teacher "does" once that person arrives in a classroom. Further, the strong discourses of testing and accountability can drown out even the strongest intent to "do better" for the students in our classrooms. Therefore, and as I continue to suggest in this book, I am inclined to consider a course of instruction for what it can offer students in the moments of the learning encounter, given that the effects of coursework in teacher education are far from clear (Cochran-Smith *et al.*, 2012). In the Fall of 2011 I decided for the first time to use Toni Morrison's *Beloved* in a social studies methods and curriculum course. The novel, just as teacher education, specifically, and formal spaces of pedagogy more generally, does not necessarily meet comfortable expectations. Expectations, rather, are defied through the narration of a terrifying history in ways that displace certainty and place it just out of reach. It was that displacing of certainty, the need for prolonged interpretation, that seemed so attractive to me, in addition to the manner in which *Beloved* intervenes in the taken-for-granted ways of historical thinking.

Beloved, among other things, introduces the conceptualization of the ways in which the past inhabits and occupies the present, something that research in teacher education has long struggled to do. In the novel, the past occupies the present as terrifying reminders of systemic racial violence felt in devastatingly personal ways. We are invited to know the past with particular intimacy. In teacher education, we come to know the figure of the teacher's past as their "apprenticeship of observation" (Lortie, 1975) and, thus, our role as teacher educators is to separate (in order to call into questions) their prior knowledge from their "new" knowledge. In both cases (though I am careful here to note that I am not making direct comparisons between slavery and learning to teach), the reworking of the relationships between past and present brings trouble.

Difficult Knowledge and Full Speech

One of the contributions that psychoanalytic theory brings to the pedagogical arena is the idea that significant learning, learning that makes a difference, is felt as an imposition as often as it is felt to be liberation. One of the frustrating features of significant learning is that it more often introduces the learner into greater senses of not-knowing and a greater realm of uncertainty and complexity than stability and simplicity. This is particularly true of learning that involves the reconfiguration of what had previously counted as "lovely" knowledge (see chapter 3); knowledge that can give way to a new narration of the self, the world, and the relationships between the two (Pitt & Britzman, 2003). Upon the encounter with an experience in which the learner is asked, or compelled, to confront and revise those ready-made versions that no longer seem sufficient, all sorts of affective reactions are instantiated.

The frustrations arising from the experience of pedagogical interventions into normative ways of thinking may arise in all sorts of pedagogical spaces. They can occur in the face of the museum visit that confounds or resists narrative closure (Ellsworth, 2005), or those that fail to play the part of the traditional exhibit authorizing a dominant story of show and tell (Willinsky, 1998). Of course, they can occur in classrooms or theaters or street corners. One specific scene of pedagogy in which these kinds of affective manifestations occur is when the subject matter of social breakdown and massive trauma is the object of learning.

The literature on difficult knowledge takes great care in relating the pedagogical present to the traumatic past and delineates the terms of that tense relationship. What I have come to understand about difficult knowledge is extended by the Lacanian notion of "full speech." I turn to this Lacanian concept here because of the ways it adds an account of possible futures to the conversation of difficult knowledge. Full speech "reorders past contingencies by conferring in them the sense of *necessities to come*, such as they are constituted by the scant freedom through which the subject makes them present" (Lacan, 2006, p. 213, emphasis mine). In other words, the learner is confronting a particular thought or object in the present in which prior ways of knowing are revised for the purposes of some kind of future use. It kicks the footing from beneath the ladder of knowledge or the linear progression of development. Full speech is analyzed not in terms of the content of what is communicated but in terms of what "difference this knowledge makes" (Felman, 1987, p. 56). Lacan acknowledges that full speech is not a feature of everyday life but rather a phenomenon that results from a particular kind of intervention into the empty speech of the patient (2006, p. 208). It is an ideational exchange that makes a demand. The analyst must wait through, must listen, but not act upon, the "empty speech"—that which communicates nothing other than regimented ways of knowing—of the analysand and then offer an intervention that helps the analysand see his or her world from a different vantage point. It allows for new and forward thinking, rather than recursive or past looking thought.

Difficult knowledge invites and may even produce the kind of knowledge that can lead to the breakdown of our ideas about what will be safe, what will be certain, and what will be open for new ways of knowing (Britzman, 2000). In this sense it has the same kind of forward-looking feature as carried in the notion of "full speech." As such, "difficult knowledge" is a condition, a function of a particular kind of pedagogical intervention, and is comprised of a particular relationship to knowledge. Lacan's "full speech," as I understand its relation to difficult knowledge, is another way to conceptualize the creative and productive potentialities imbedded within this tumultuous process. But what could be productive about such potentially painful confrontations with knowledge?

Such a confrontation can be considered potentially generative because "knowledge is worth just as much as it costs, a pretty penny, in that it takes elbow grease and that it's difficult" (Lacan, 1999, p. 97). The crux of the problem with seemingly new and significant knowledge is that "the difficulty of its exercise is the very thing that is increasing the difficulty of its acquisition" (p. 97). What this means is that a facet of the difficulty of difficult knowledge is in trying to come to grips with its exercise, or to put it more colloquially, its use value. What I mean here is that students in my experience will frequently ask, "What are we supposed to do?" about the particular issue being confronted. This is an exceedingly difficult question in which there is often little that can be done. It means that part of the difficulty of difficult knowledge is settling into that which is disquieting. It may also mean that the more difficult an idea is to conceptualize as being able to immediately deploy in the world, the more difficult that idea is to conceptualize at all. Because of this, it becomes all the more easy to dismiss that not-yet-considered thing as a toss-away, as "bad" knowledge, not relevant, or useless, and it becomes folded in the wrinkled relations of ignorance and knowledge (Felman, 1987). Ideas are not always dismissed, though, and learners will be enticed to reach back and forth with their attachments to knowledge. To exemplify the ways in which present, past, and future get tangled in proximity to the pedagogical scenes of difficult knowledge, I turn to one of my students' responses to her reading of *Beloved*:

> A story like *Beloved* would come with a trigger warning on the feminist internet. A trigger warning before a post serves as a heads up to the traumatized, the emotionally fragile, the tender-hearted, and the survivors among us. It is a warning that tells you what lies ahead and to proceed at your own risk.

This particular student's writing highlights a feature of difficult knowledge; that difficult knowledge is not only an individually felt "thing," but it anticipates what happens upon further circulation of it and is contingent upon some sort of intervention. In other words, we know that proceeding will likely cause some pain. Bringing such a stance into formal spaces of education requires some care: these are dangerous and unwieldy ideas. These ideas are always present, the stance on offer here centers and acknowledges their danger and suggests that without such confrontation, the dangers are even greater. The student's writing also shares a feature of full speech, in that the articulation of the student looks forward; it anticipates a future and alludes to the acknowledgment or interpretation that actions be taken anew, on behalf of others, and for some measure of thoughtful protection of fragile subjectivities. It acknowledges the past of those traumatized but does not prevent or preclude their exposure; it seeks to make it more tolerable. It does not reduce difficulty, though its experience is forecast and is therefore made visible and seems to indicate a kind of utility that has been attained through some type of affective struggle.

In the case of *Beloved*, a book that is dedicated to the "sixty million and more" dead as a result of the slave trade, the question (the question of "use-value again) becomes "What now"? The dedication, the reading, the painful encounter with the narrative does nothing to bring back those lost. Reading *Beloved* will no more change the absence of those millions of slaves than my visiting the United States Holocaust Museum will return the murdered Jews to their descendants. The use of the knowledge of these terrifying histories and the experience of equally terrifying affective responses to them can only be understood as healthy if there is a concurrent invitation to bring learners into conversations about how that knowledge may call them to question assumptions about themselves, the world, and the relationships between the two.

That invitation indicates another feature of difficult knowledge, and that is the manner in which the terms upon which one would qualify the knowledge is not the discrete "bit" but rather what is said about it (Lacan, 1999, p. 96). Of course remembrance and memorialization serve crucial socio-political and psychic functions. What education theorists and researchers have shown is, though, is that perhaps the most important feature of engaging with texts that provoke this difficult estrangement is not simply or only to learn about the historical events represented (Simon, Rosenberg & Eppert, 2000). Rather, the idea is also that these particular kinds of texts can allow for a manner of "collective symbolizing" that allow readers the opportunity to rejoin their psychic and affective postures with the sociality of language within a community (Tarc, 2011b). This may be stated otherwise as the distinction between learning about and learning from (Britzman, 1998). Or, as Felman (1987) writes, "knowledge cannot be exchanged, it has to be used" (p. 81). In this case, knowledge cannot dwell in the moments of the past that cannot be redeemed, nor even revisited. Knowledge must be narrated and re-narrated. What seems to attract researchers in this area is that the affects that are produced in relationship to the objects of learning are crucially important features of the psychic life of a teacher, and, I think, in this sense that the interactions are worth the pretty penny.

Reading *Beloved* as Pedagogical Text

> There is no place you or I can go, to think about or not think about, to summon the presences of, or recollect the absences of slaves; nothing that reminds us of the ones who made the journey and of those who did not make it. There is no suitable memorial or plaque or wreath or wall or park or skyscraper lobby. There's no three-hundred-foot-tower. There's no small bench by the road. There is not even a tree scored, an initial that I can visit or you can visit in Charleston or Savannah or New York or Providence or, better still on the banks of the Mississippi. And because such a place doesn't exist (that I know of), the book had to. (Morrison, 1989)

Toni Morrison calls us to question the structures of memory and memorialization. The physical structures of museums and other commemorating architectures are put in tension with an absence. That those structures, buildings, and plaques exist to memorialize also serves as evidence of those that do not; memorials commemorating those long since dead as a result of slavery. That there is no bench by the road is not only an indictment of the non-existence of physical artifacts to attest to the atrocities of slavery in the United States, the statement also indicts the lack of socio-cultural narratives and discourses that would invent and construct such memorials. It also is offered as the justification for the authoring of *Beloved*, in which the past is re-memorialized, narra-tivized through the subjective location of the former slave, the slave himself, herself, and through the physical and psychical manifestation of a murdered child. The novel is written as a memorial. This memorial, this bench by the road, is less restful than furtive, less calming than provocative. As much as any equipment or strategy the reader needs to work through the pages, the reader must first forego their ready-made stances toward history and indeed toward learning. The text serves as an intervention, though often difficult to immediately understand.

What a reader encounters in the pages of *Beloved* is a narrative in which understanding is difficult. It is not as though the words in *Beloved* are difficult to understand; rather the murder of one's own child (infanticide is the knot around which the narrative winds) is so horrific that the reader struggles to comprehend. The story is brutally violent but is the polar opposite of the gra-tuitous representations of violence that circulate widely in popular media. It is a representation of the ways that complicated and difficult histories have a bearing on the present, something that in social studies and history education (the formal pedagogical spaces in which I work) is a difficult, but crucial, con-cept to introduce to students.

Beloved is a novel spun around interrelated themes of memory, trauma, maternity, violence, property, and historiography. As it relates to memorial-ization, *Beloved* is a text that demonstrates "a tension between needing to bury the past and an equally necessary forgetting" (Rushdy, 1999, p. 39). In terms of its pedagogy, "the teaching" in/of the novel "proceeds through a listening, a non-telling, a non-mastery, in each layer" of it (Edgerton, 1993, p. 220). The narrative is loosely based upon the case of Margaret Garner, an escaped slave who murdered her daughter to prevent her return to slavery. But Morrison "radically calls into question traditional conceptions of history, language, and subjectivity, while it makes a call to America to remember repressed moments of its past" (Samuels 2001, p. 123). It "reconceptualizes American history" (Krumholtz, 1999, p. 107) by narrating the institution of slavery from well beyond the narrative tropes of western historiography. Instead Morrison cre-ates a narrative from within the African consciousness and draws on African tradition as well as modernist literary strategies to tell her story. Here, the his-tory project is not to arrive at the dispassionate truth, rather to take the reader within the experiences of slavery. The book is intended to function as the stand-in for adequate memorializing practices. As in the case of the use-value of difficult knowledge, the function of the conjuring of the past in a particular way is meant to have an impact on the present as well as a future usefulness. The "bench by the side of the road" is not just meant to be a structure, it is a structure that is meant to be utilized. The bench, I might say, is meant to be "full speech."

Beloved is about slavery, emancipation, maternity, love, memory, trauma, redemption, and forgetting. Beloved, the title character, is the physical representation of trauma. Beloved, whose given name we are never given, is the third-born child of the main character, Sethe. Born in slavery and subject to the Fugitive Slave Act, Sethe murders this third-born child by slicing her throat as the character called "Schoolteacher" arrives to reclaim his property. We learn early in the novel that "Beloved" is the only word etched on to her gravestone because it was all for which Sethe could barter the engraver, the exchanged currency being yet again her body. Recollecting this exchange and the anger and pain harbored in the child's soul, we read:

> Who would have thought at little old baby could harbor so much rage? Rutting among the stones under the eyes of the engraver's son was not enough. Not only did she have to live out her years in a house palsied by the baby's fury at having its throat cut, but those ten minutes she spent pressed up against dawn-colored stone studded with star chips, her knees as open as the grave, were longer than life, more alive, more pulsating than the baby blood that soaked her fingers like oil. (pp. 5–6)

In this short selection we are presented with the murder of the baby, the way that the figure of the baby now haunts Sethe's present, and how the exchange of her body for recollection figures in her memory of committing the murderous act. Not yet do we know much else. It isn't until much later in the novel that the full circumstances of the infanticide are revealed. And so it is only in our return to these opening pages are we able to understand the full articulation of those words. As one of my students wrote: "I had to read a few of these passages two or three times to fully understand everything that was going on (granted, this happened throughout most of the book)." As a point of reference related to this felt need to read and re-read because of the degree to which the text defies immediate understanding, when Morrison was told by Oprah Winfrey that the text was so difficult that she felt like she had to read it twice, Morrison responded, "That my dear, is called reading."

What a reader encounters on their first and subsequent readings is range of characters that we come to know in various settings and times and through a variety of perspectives. We come to know the lives of the male slaves in the presence of the lone single female slave; the ways in which being property is dehumanizing and violent despite being the presence of a benevolent master. We come to know a character we only know as "Schoolteacher" as the hyper-rational embodiment of racist enlightenment thought who teaches his nephews to list the human and animal traits of the slaves in different columns on a page (with ink in their pens produced by the very slaves they are describing, and largely considering as, animals). We also come to know Schoolteacher's lesson: that power "belongs to the definers and not to the defined" (p. 225). We come to know Paul D., the lone surviving male from "Sweet Home" (the name of the plantation), and his escape from slavery, and his testimony of the tragic end of the lives of the other slaves, including Sethe's husband Paul A., whose body is mutilated and hanged from a tree. We come to know how the community ostracized Sethe, her grandmother Baby Suggs, and her daughter Denver for 18 years. The novel, in its end, as Eppert (2003) has noted, is as much about forgetting as it is about remembering and memorializing the past.

That a mother murdered her infant to avoid returning her to slavery is scary enough—that the way that particular act, committed under the auspices of both the rationality of the Fugitive Slave Act as well as under the influence of a strange maternal protection—that the act worked in the sense of Schoolteacher going back without his property—I feel as though all of this has a significance for how we even begin to think about learning from the past whether this learning occurs on a city bus, in a museum, or a classroom.

Re-cognizing and Reading *Beloved* and/in Teacher Education

In my theorizing of reading *Beloved* in a methods course, there is a doubled problem of recognition. Recognition alludes to the familiar but difficult to place and calls forth a need to think again. The first problem relates to the curricular choices that confront students with challenging "difficult" texts and the degree to which such confrontations elicit a felt need to rethink, reconsider, re-cognize. Difficult knowledge involves a reach back in time, but what is grasped in that reach is far from being certain to feel solid, clean, or appropriate to lift and carry forth. This is to say that the stuff from which we are expected to build a future may seem flimsy or even rotten. In holding these residuals of trauma, students may or may not recognize their own affective reactions to such narratives as they struggle to make sense of what seems beyond comprehension (i.e., systematic violence, genocide, infanticide). Sandlos (2010), drawing upon Freud's elucidation of the "uncanny," focuses on the question of the reader's "capacity to tolerate an emotional experience with uncertainty in relation to the object" (p. 62). Although Sandlos' work discusses cinematic depictions of violence in schools (the object of inquiry being Van Sant's film *Elephant*) and the degree to which those representations require the viewer to make a meaning, Morrison's novel similarly makes a demand on the reader. These difficult demands are often not welcome, but the ways in which students respond to those demands may fall along a wide spectrum of reactions. Resistance, Britzman (2010) reminds us, will prompt the learner to reach out for meanings, but that "things do not add up; even as thought events escalate, they only leave in their wake defeated equations" (p. 244). In *Beloved*, then, the content of breakdown and loss may relate to a sense in which a reader may feel themselves to be broken down, reaching for meanings that don't feel too steady. While this may initially seem to be somewhat of a sticking-place that we ought avoid, it may also "evoke for the viewer [a] desire for a more intimate relation to historical reality" (Sandlos, 2010, p. 64). In this sense, the possibility for recognition (for re-thinking) is a hopeful, though perhaps not smooth, one.

In *Beloved*, readers are invited into a narrative composed from within the logic of the slave-as-person, the individuals whose lives were being lived through the tumultuousness of slavery, escape, and emancipation. When the reader is a future social studies teacher, such an invitation presses upon the capacity to recognize historical content. *Beloved* presents those who will be teachers with history what is not what they think history should be like. Within social studies education, a prevailing stance toward how students should learn history is as though they are historians in training: a rational critique of evidence that it uses to support verifiable accounts of the past. *Beloved* is a novel in which we are invited to be in an encounter with history. As a history text we get lessons, and to illustrate this idea I'll provide an excerpt illuminating the time of post-emancipation. While the Emancipation Proclamation ended slavery in most accounts, the institution persisted. In a passage describing this, Morrison writes:

> The war had been over for 5 years then, but nobody white or black seemed to know it. Odd clusters and strays of Negroes wandered the back roads and cowpaths from Schenectady to Jackson. Dazed but insistent, they searched each other out for word of a cousin, an aunt, a friend who once said, "Call on me. Anytime you get near Chicago, just call on me." Some of them are running from family that could not support them, some to family, some were running from dead crops, dead kin, life threats, and

took-over land. Boys younger than Buglar and Howard; configurations and blends of families of women and children, while elsewhere solitary, hunted and hunting for, were men, men, men. Forbidden public transportation, chased by debt and filthy "talking sheets," they followed secondary routes, scanned the horizon for signs and counted heavily on each other. Silent, except for social courtesies, when they met one another they neither described nor asked about the sorrow that drove them from one place to another. The whites didn't bear speaking on. Everybody knew. (p. 63)

In this selection, what is commonly referenced as the "great migration" in US history textbooks is told in a tale of sadness. It is made of wandering, escaping, desperate, dangerous—not some progressing narrative of betterment. And we see mentioned at the end of this passage, the white subjectivity othered. It is yet another example where there is a challenge to recognize the history of a particular experience in a way that may not fit, as such, as an historical text. What historical novels can do, Berlant (2011) writes is to allow readers to inhabit "the affective life of a past moment" and also to "create distance from the present moment" (p. 66). This kind of shifting of proximity and distance indicates that the form of the novel functions to do something that historical texts cannot. That something, though, which is the experience of imagining from within a past moment that disturbs or displaces the current moment, is something from within which social studies educators might recognize a pedagogical opportunity. In this case, it is recognizing the limits of traditional or conventional historical texts and the potential for texts that enhance and challenge our comfortable ways of knowing and being in classrooms.

The second plane of recognition, the one that is felt no matter the content of the course, has to do with the preoccupation of those learning to teach. Student teachers seem to be preoccupied with their experience in schools and devote their thinking to those who populate the subject position relegated as the ones who learn. Britzman (2012) has described the scene of student teaching as one in which the adult returns to adolescence (adolescents) in order to either replay or repair their own histories of learning (p. 273). The estranging experience of encountering the profound dramas of loss, illusion, love, guilt, pain—and their opposites—that comprise much of the adolescent experience are matched by the estranging experiences of going back to school, this time as a grown-up. While reading of social trauma within the conceptual confines of difficult knowledge and memorializing makes us "go back" to those times of infant helplessness, going back to high school, now at the mercy of the signifier "teacher" or "student-teacher," is disorienting along the same axis. It's an instance of repetition. This is to say that the experience where one would expect to find familiarity but is met with a frustrated sense of misrecognition, occurs no matter what we have students read in our classrooms. As soon as they begin whatever form of practicum experience their program requires, they are thrown into what should seem normal but now seems absurd, confusing, outrageous, terrible, boring, and not good enough. Now armed with some university knowledge of what they think a good teacher ought to be up to, students come back to the university embodying a certain disarray. In reading *Beloved*, and in returning to the schoolroom, the tensions between the past and its imprint on our present are there; and they are making a mess of things. In short, the experience of learning to teach, just as the experience of reading *Beloved*, is marked by misrecognition.

Reading. Britzman (2009) figures that reading "teaches us a lesson we already know, that we cannot let go of affected life" (p. 58). In reference to Morrison's work in *Beloved*, though, what we already know is being written anew—the history of slavery. This makes the grasp on affected life all the more insistent because the reading refuses to be pinned down.

In reading *Beloved* we are accessing a language that points to difficult knowledge; it both illustrates and evokes breakdown. Morrison takes the reader into new terrain by telling old stories in new ways, ways that seem unfamiliar, but seem difficult, seem not to initially make sense. "What her novel does, as does good pedagogy generally, is to call into question knowledge that claims to be its own authority" (Edgerton, 1993, p. 224). As Lacan has suggested, "the only true teaching is that which provokes the desire to know in its listeners" (ibid). Following Edgerton's work regarding the literary as a model for pedagogy, though, there is still the problem of desire to not know—that other side of knowledge in the position of ignorance. Literature not only calls into question self-evident knowledge, but it can often instantiate a vehement defense of those same sets of knowledge. The value, then, of engaging a pedagogy that provokes is located in the degree to which the object, the text, allows the subject to narrate their lives in new ways.

Tarc (2011b) argues for "a particular of engagement with literature that can give readers insight into the interpretive practice we use to understand how we read and write social realities we live and live out with and on the bodies of others" (p. 65). Tarc continues to acknowledge that this particular kind of engagement is often forsaken in favor of one of the more common ones in classrooms—one that focuses on the more steady components of a text, the obvious content and the structure of the story. *Beloved*, though, has no steady component. It puts the reader in a position where they are forced to have questions, and, and as my students and Oprah indicated, read again. This is, of course, by Morrison's (1988) design, who in speaking about the first two sentences of *Beloved*, said,

> I wanted that sudden feeling of being snatched up and thrown into that house, precisely the way they were. They were picked up from anywhere at any time, and removed without resources, without defenses, without anything. Naked. They had each other, they had a little music and had the urgency of the task at hand. So that is what the reader has. (p. 45)

As a reader approaches *Beloved*, then, they are intentionally being pulled outside of their subject location. Estrangement is the desired effect. The reader, by Morrison's design, is estranged from their expectation of what it means to read and to learn history.

Aesthetic Conflict in Encountering the Historical Novel

In social studies education there may be more to conflicts than just competing accounts or new vistas from which to consider a social or historical event. The conflict can also light the fires of our own anxious thoughts of relations and worries about our place in the world. Psychoanalysts name these affective consequences elements of "aesthetic conflict" (Britzman, 2006; Meltzer & Williams, 1998), which is the idea that evocative texts do not only evoke ambiguous thoughts about historical events or social contexts, they will simultaneously beckon us toward our interior lives of uncertainty and ambiguity as well. What this means is that our engagements in social studies education with film, photograph, and literature aids in a provocative way our thinking about more than just the world "out there." As Britzman (2006) explains, "aesthetic conflict is needed for thinking to matter" (p. 22). But aesthetic conflict beckons the teacher and learner toward new ways of being with one another in the world because of the way the conflict necessitates a working through of those meanings through language. Aesthetic conflict, a term brought forward by Meltzer and Williams (1998) to represent "the aesthetic impact of the outside of the beautiful mother, available to the senses, and the enigmatic inside which must be construed by creative imagination" (p. 22). An aesthetic object, we might say, is that which prompts, invites, compels, or instantiates a conflict between the "knowable"—or sayable—and the uncanny, more difficult or even impossible to narrate in the world. Karyn Sandlos (2009) writes about the aesthetic object as opening "dilemmas of interpretation and meaning making and so may be experienced as threatening to the inner organization of the self" (p. 66). To illustrate this idea, I turn to part of my study of reading *Beloved* with social studies teachers: the part where they read the first two sentence of the novel without context.

What I wanted to know is whether or not I could make a research study out of the question of how teachers deal with uncertainty, deal with the interior conflicts instantiated by difficult knowledge of living in the twenty-first century, and confront confusion. The study I wanted to carry out was truncated for reasons out of my control (see the preface), but I was able to engage in conversations with participants about this opening passage of *Beloved*. I handed participants the novel before they had a chance to read it and asked them what those first sentences could mean. I asked them to read the first two sentences out loud and then talk about what they thought they meant.

Each of the responses was different, of course, but taken together I think they represent something of a splintering of meaning as initial moments of difficulty. Their responses underscore the pedagogical effectiveness of Morrison's desire to "snatch up" the reader and throw them into disarray. Many participants talked about how a venomous baby seemed difficult to imagine.

> And it (laughs) describes the baby having venom which isn't what we typically think of when you think of a baby. And I guess it possesses that baby's venom? How could they—how could something so new be so spiteful? We kind of associate that with age or experience. And the baby is the "tabula rasa" you know it's not supposed to be spiteful…hate is for—you have to be a little bit older to start hating.

In this response the newness of the baby and the oldness of the house become conflated. So too do hate, spite, and venom. If we do not think of a baby with venom, then the question is forced: "How could something so new be so spiteful?" That is a disoriented understanding. Below, a different participant's response reveals similar themes, that babies are innocent and so the description she read in *Beloved* defies comprehension. Similarly, her own description defies clear understandings a she reaches toward articulation:

> "Full of a baby's venom," oh yeah, like—but the baby like—the fact that baby has venom. I'm like what…I can't even comprehend. Like a devil child. The devil child. A poisonous child. But it's hard for me to imagine a baby, you know, having some sort of venom that just…I can't imagine…it just doesn't go together to me …because you don't know yet if the—that they venom. You don't know that until they're older.

Maybe it's not human. Could it be a snake? So, full of venom, …obviously 124 and the babies, hum, then I'm, it's almost like this baby hurt this person somehow like an unwanted baby…I don't know now I'm really excited about reading this.

In this reader's reaction, I interpret statement's from a person who is willing to follow and express her train of thought and make associations as they come to mind. Some sentences begin and are not completed. There are shifts in address from first to second person and back to first person again. These associations allude to biblical images of the devil and snakes and also articulate a host of negations of knowledge: "I can't comprehend," "it's hard for me to imagine," "I can't imagine," "it doesn't go together," "you don't know," "I don't know."

Other participants wondered if perhaps the baby had a disease, speculated about sexual and emotional abuse, the cuddliness of babies, the way they are "supposed to be," and predicted that something bad had and is also about to happen. What occurs on our first reading is indicative, I theorize, of our encounters with first readings of other spaces when they do not meet our expectations. From all of this I can conclude that Morrison's intentions in writing were provocative of an affective response that unsettled narrative expectations. But what good is that for a social studies teacher's education?

Students have said that "the book was confusing," or "written in a confusing way" rather than stating that they needed to think about it in order to come to some understanding. Either way, the experience of reading the text exists in a location outside of expectation. Students share similar desires in regard to their experiences in schools and in reading *Beloved*. One of these desires is that "it"—the object of experience—rather than themselves are the ones in need of change. However, it is the teacher education program, the course, the host teacher, or the students who must do the changing in order for the "proper" learning to occur. It is an outwardly directed desire that is manifested in relation to that same sense of estrangement which, put colloquially, sounds like, "what the heck is going on here? I was not prepared for this."

And similarly, when a reader comes to read *Beloved*, they very well could say that their education and reading had not prepared them for this. Now that the narrative looks differently, now that the subjectivities are represented without punctuation and with shifting pronouns signifying their thoughts and actions, and that the boundaries between past and present in violence and care are blurred, we don't know what to do with this or that. It provides the conditions for misrecognition. But perhaps in not recognizing some things we are allowed to recognize other. Perhaps in not thinking the predominant thoughts of doctrinal versions of social studies education, for example, one is able to think thoughts in a new relation to pedagogy, in ways that move toward more human and ethical ways of relating within the pedagogical situation. One of my students, an African American woman from rural Arkansas, writing about *Beloved*, demonstrates this kind of recognition:

> [When I read *Beloved*]I think of the kids I know, my sisters, my cousins, and their friends in high school, and the things that they deal with. I think of the kid I used to be and the girls I used to go to school with and I consider how hard reading a book like *Beloved* would be. This is the kind of hard that would have nothing to do with reading ability or willingness to do the work. This is the kind of hard that knows. *Beloved* speaks to that kind of knowledge.

"The kind of hard that knows," it should be noted, is another way of stating that difficulty of difficult knowledge which is found within the burden, felt in the present, of reaching back to the past. And it is not just the past referenced in the text; it is the personal past elicited in the encounter with it. This articulation of difficult knowledge works on a doubled plane of memory: on the one hand, there is the memory of her own schooling, and on the other, the ways in which the entirety of this statement relates to the encounter with the traumatic memories of slavery. Yet this student's writing also points and moves forward, as in the condition of full speech, because her references to these people from her past are articulated as possible futures.

Conclusion

In my teaching of *Beloved* in a social studies methods course, I set out to create a pedagogical space that shared component features with learning to teach and structure a "scene of address" (Ellworth, 1997) that invites students into an experience of being at odds with expectations. Morrison's *Beloved* does just that; it performs a pedagogy that intentionally estranges. It acknowledges that only by reworking the coordinates by which understanding is navigated can changes be made that result in an adequate address of the tumultuous past. This navigation of shifting coordinates, relating past to present, is difficult knowledge. My understanding of difficult knowledge is extended with the Lacanian idea of "full speech," that put simply indicates a change in understanding that leads to seemingly new avenues of thought.

But this isn't just an essay about social studies and teacher education. This essay considers the scene of teacher education where students are tasked with simultaneously grappling with the traumatic residuals of social past and the changing subject position between student and teacher. The way I think of the work of the teacher educator and the student teacher is something of an odd dance in which the teacher educator is in some ways facilitating a re-cognition and attempting to help the will-be-teacher into new ways of know-ing an old scene. Ellsworth (1997), drawing on the psychoanalytic relation, has described this recognition as changing

> Not only what the patient "knows"—it can change how the patient knows it. It can change the patient's relation to what she knows. It can change what she does with what she knows, how she experiences what she knows. (p. 69)

Ellsworth is remarking on the ways that shifting relations to knowledge set a productive relationship to it in motion. This kind of recognition in the work of teacher education shares a feature of "full speech" in that it is an act arising from an intervention such that old meanings are refashioned for new times. But that intervention may feel rather disagreeable during the initial time of learning. In this sense it shares the features of difficult knowledge.

As a final note, only half of my students came to class on the day that *Beloved* was to be initially discussed. I interpreted this is a strange when, during the rest of the semester, no more than 2 students were absent during any given session. In the fact of my stating, in the subsequent session, how odd I found it that half the class was gone, students responded with their own stories of illness, of family obligation, and of having not read the assigned material. This helps me conclude that, as a pedagogue, the novel felt simultaneously too much and too little: too much of a bother in terms of the ways it displaces the reader, and too little by way of apparent connection to the practices of becoming a teacher. Maybe there was too much of my own investment in the difficulties of approaching such devastating traumas in literature and a wishful longing to engage others in the process of engaging learning in that way. And similarly too little by way of pedagogical guidance toward meaning. On the other hand, if pedagogy is in some way mobilized by the need to reach for meanings, then I can at least take small satisfaction and feel comfortable continuing to structure similar pedagogical scenes.

References

Britzman, D. P. (1998). *Lost subjects, contested objects: Toward a psychoanalytic inquiry of learning*. Albany: SUNY Press.

Britzman, D. P. (2000). If the story cannot end: Deferred action, ambivalence, and difficult knowledge. In R. I. Simon, S. Rosenberg & C. Eppert (Eds.), *Between hope and despair: Pedagogy and the remembrance of historical trauma*. Lanham, MD: Rowman & Littlefield.

Britzman, D. P. (2003a). *Practice makes practice: A critical study of learning to teach*. Albany, NY: SUNY Press.

Britzman, D. P. (2003b). *After-education: Anna Freud, Melanie Klein, and psychoanalytic histories of learning*. Albany, NY: SUNY Press.

Britzman, D.P. (2006). *Novel education: Psychoanalytic studies of learning and not learning*. New York, NY: Peter Lang.

Britzman, D.P. (2009). *The very thought of education: Psychoanalysis and the impossible professions*. Albany, NY: SUNY Press.

Britzman, D. P. (2010). Some psychoanalytic observation on quiet, ordinary and painful resistance. *International Journal of Leadership in Education, 13*(3), 239–248.

Britzman, D. P. (2012). The adolescent teacher: A psychoanalytic note on regression in the professions. *Journal of Infant, Child and Adolescent Psychotherapy, 11*(3), 272–283.

Cochran-Smith, M., Cannady, M., McEachern, K., Mitchell, K., Piazza, P., Power, C., & Ryan, A. (2012). Teachers' education and outcomes: Mapping the research terrain. *Teachers College Record, 114*(10), 1–49.

Edgerton, S. H. (1993). Toni Morrison teaching the interminable. In C. McCarthy & W. Critchlow (Eds.), *Race, identity and representation in education* (pp. 220–235). New York, NY: Routledge.

Ellsworth, E. A. (1997). *Teaching positions: Difference, pedagogy, and the power of address*. New York, NY: Teachers College Press.

Ellsworth, E. A. (2005). *Places of learning: Media, architecture, pedagogy*. New York, NY: RoutledgeFarmer.

Eppert, C. (2003). Histories re-imagined, forgotten and forgiven: Student responses to Toni Morrison's *Beloved*. *Changing English, 10*, 185–194.

Farley, L. (2009). Radical hope: or, the problem of uncertainty in history education. *Curriculum Inquiry, 39*(4), 537–554.

Felman, S. (1987). *Jacques Lacan and the adventure of insight: Psychoanalysis in contemporary culture*. Cambridge, MA: Harvard University Press.

Krumholtz (1992). The ghosts of slavery: Historical recovery in Toni Morrison's *Beloved*. In W. L. Andrews & N. Y. McKay (Eds.), *Toni Morrison's* Beloved: *A Casebook* (pp. 107–126). New York, NY: Oxford University Press.

Lacan, J. (2006). *Ecrits: The first complete edition in English*. New York, NY: Norton.

Lacan, J. (1999). *On feminine sexuality, the limits of love and knowledge: The Seminar of Jacques Lacan, Book XX, Encore*. B. Fink (Trans). New York, NY: Norton.

Lortie, D. (1975). *Schoolteacher: A sociological study*. Chicago: University of Chicago Press.

Matthews, S. (2009). Hitler's car as curriculum text: Reading adolescents reading history. *Journal of the Canadian Association for Curriculum Studies, 7*(2), 49–85.

Meltzer, D., & Williams, M.H. (1988). *The apprehension of beauty: The role of aesthetic conflict in development*. London, UK: Karnac.

Morrison, T. (1987) *Beloved*. New York: Random House.

Morrison, T. (1988). A bench by the road: *Beloved* by Toni Morrison. In C.C. Denard (Ed.), *Toni Morrison: Conversations*. Jackson, MS: University Press of Mississippi.

Pitt, A. J., & Britzman, D. P. (2003). Speculations on qualities of difficult knowledge in teaching and learning: An experiment in psychoanalytic research. *International Journal of Qualitative Studies in Education, 16*(6), 755–776.

Rushdy, A. H. A. (1999). Daughters signifyin(g) history: The example of Toni Morrison's *Beloved*. In W. L. Andrews & N. Y. McKay (Eds.), *Toni Morrison's Beloved: A Casebook* (pp. 37–66). New York, NY: Oxford University Press.

Samuels, R. (2001). *Writing prejudices: The psychoanalysis and pedagogy of discrimination from Shakespeare to Toni Morrison*. Albany, NY: SUNY Press.

Sandlos, K. (2010). Encounters with insignificance in teaching and learning: Gus Van Sant's *Elephant. The Review of Education, Pedagogy & Cultural Studies, 31*(1), 55–73.

Simon, R.I. (2011). A shock to thought: Curatorial judgement and the public exhibition of "difficult knowledge". *Memory Studies, 4*(4), 432–449.

Simon, R. I. (2014). *A pedagogy of witnessing: Curatorial practice and the pursuit of social justice*. Albany, NY: SUNY Press.

Simon, R.I, Rosenberg, S., & Eppert, C. (2000). *Between hope and despair: Pedagogy and remembrance of historical trauma*. Lanham, MD: Rowman & Littlefield.

Tarc, A. M. (2011a). Reparative curriculum. *Curriculum Inquiry, 41*(3), 350–372.

Tarc, A. M. (2011b). Disturbing reading: J.M. Coetzee's "The Problem of Evil." *Changing English, 18*(1), 57–66.

Willinsky, J. (1998). *Learning to divide the world: Education at empire's end*. Minneapolis: University of Minnesota Press.

· 6 ·

QUESTIONS AND PERSPECTIVES IN SOCIAL STUDIES EDUCATION

Much of the material in the preceding chapters elaborates various difficulties in learning. For social studies education, these difficulties need urgent solutions because of the degree to which our relations with others in the world depend on the ways in which we organize our reactions to what we encounter therein. How do we come to understand the complicated world in which we live? What do ideas do to us and what does that doing mean for what we think of as our responsibility to and with others? Difficult knowledge is a relation from which these questions arise. Questions may be our best currency as teachers and researchers. They serve as provocations and invitations toward thinking and re-thinking. When we encounter a text, idea, representation, or thought that challenges a dominant narrative or offers a new one, when a vantage is offered that unsettles a thought, difficult knowledge is found in that current scene of knowing and relation. One way in which we can locate and work with difficult knowledge is through a focus on, and engagement with, the questions that arise in engagement with the world.

I'll begin this chapter by tracing various movements of knowledge as they play out in relationship to one particular question as an example of the relationship between questions, perspectives, and difficult knowledge. This question "Why didn't I know this before?" is articulated in relation to knowledge that has caused a significant change in the consideration of a facet of previously stable understandings. I use that question as an example of the ways in which questions function and the ways in which they can continue to be a productive pre-occupation for social studies teachers and researchers.

This chapter, like the previous one, is located in and around social studies methods courses. Anxieties abound there. Common questions arise in the curious time when students are not only students but also not yet credentialed teachers. This time is spent in university classrooms with people like me, people who are committed to inviting prospective teachers into a pedagogical practice that takes social and political justice into account. "Can I teach this stuff to my students? What if students are not motivated? If a parent is upset with my teaching, will I be fired?" There are well-trained conundrums between theory and practice, between the methods course and the high school classroom. University classroom knowledge is questioned in terms of its use value. In the university classroom we attend to differences of linguistic, racial, economic, and religious natures as we consider the ramifications about what it is that we do. We address the possibilities for creating unit and lesson plans. We meet the anxiety of students who wonder whether or not they know enough. We meet the anxiety about the degree to which what they do know is legitimate content to teach to high school students: Is it too political, controversial, or critical? Is it going to result in a phone call from a parent? These are anxious moments in that they locate the worry in moments yet to come. Those who serve as instructors of methods courses will not find those interrogatives terribly novel or unfamiliar. Indeed, much of our energy in methods courses focuses on the anxieties that seem to be located in such moments.

When I teach social studies methods courses there are often situations and relations of difficult knowledge. When teaching with memoirs like *Night* (1956), or graphic novels such as *Deogratias* (2006), films like *When the Levees Broke* (2006), novels like *Beloved* (1987), or more recently discussing *Between the World and Me* (2015), there are identifiable moments when either my students or myself find each other in stuck moments, where communication becomes a burden; apologies are offered in advance of a statement; moves toward the outside of the conversation are made, and people are generally unsettled. Social studies education is precisely the location where such unsettledness can be privileged because of the degree to which most all stances focus on interpretations of multiple perspectives.

Curricular documents and scholarly work ask social studies educators to help students negotiate, among other priorities, multiple perspectives on historical and current social events. Whether this encounter with competing accounts is actualized through the interpretation of primary documents to practice "historical thinking" (Wineburg, 2001), postmodern critique (Segall, 2006; Seixas, 2001) or critical pedagogy (Kincheloe, 2001), when done well social studies provides students opportunities to examine competing narratives offering differing readings of events and processes. (den Heyer & Abbott, 2011). Indeed, in the sections in which the C3 (NCSS, 2013) outlines history education, the authors are rightly critical of a history told in a single voice. They write that "the notion of different (and often conflicting) perspectives offers a…useful idea in that it helps explain why historical actors may have interpreted what appears to be the same situation in vastly different ways" (p. 88). Issues of perspective are included in discussions about all of the social studies' disciplinary categories.

Such a stance is a clear necessity as we consider The Cold War, Vietnam, the post-Cold War nation-building projects, genocides in Rwanda and Sudan, the War on Terror, climate change, global economic fluctuations, civil rights, and current manifestations of racism are all historical events that are part of the purview of social education and that can each be accounted for in a number of different ways. They are also issues that, because of their accounting of violence and injustice, beckon the student toward situations of difficult knowledge, conflict, and controversy as I discussed in chapter three. The introduction of multiple perspectives invites questions about what happens when the alternative narrative disturbs and provokes in students a crisis of learning. It is not as though the actors in the past are the only people who have competing accounts of it. Those writing and interpreting in past, making a history or a political claim, are also offering an identifiable perspective, a partial narrative, that positions learners in particular ways.

Why didn't I know this before? Is a question that often arises across sections of a social studies methods course in which I serve as the instructor. While this question might have arisen in response to any number of texts, in this case it was articulated in response to Naomi Klein's (2008) book *The Shock Doctrine: The Rise of Disaster Capitalism*. This text was selected to invite students into conversation with an alternative narrative of events about which most students seemed to have prior knowledge. But the alternative telling, narrating, and framing of those events provoked students to ask questions of those events and their narration.

Why didn't I know this before? This question is multi-vocal. It stands out because of the ways that it implicates the self, the self's prior knowledge, the education received, and the perceived value of the information. As I discuss below, the question speaks to the content in *The Shock Doctrine* as it troubles what many students have encountered in their education. It also speaks about the ways that learning about crisis has led to its own crisis, the confrontation with a learner's own ignorance (Felman, 1982) which in this sense is a particular kind of relationship with knowledge rather than its lack. Further, the question speaks to and from an uncertainty about knowledge, particularly knowledge about social and/or historical trauma (Britzman, 1998; Farley, 2009; Matthews, 2009; Pitt & Britzman, 2003). It indicates that the use value of knowledge in the present indicts a past time when the knowledge either was not present or was differently narrativized so as to have quite different meanings. And finally this question reveals a complicated relationship between time, knowing, and pedagogy.

Here, as throughout the book, I use psychoanalytic inquiry to think about the relationships between pedagogy, trauma, vulnerability, and crisis in the contexts of social studies and teacher education. The chapters in this book all propose and explore a potential space in social studies education that can acknowledge the psychic consequences of "difficult knowledge" revealed where and when pedagogy and representations of trauma meet (Britzman, 1998). Following Farley (2009), and elaborated in the third chapter, I consider social studies education as a "site of conflict rather than its solution" (p. 538). Whereas the predominant modes of thinking in social studies education are codified along either traditional collective story or disciplinary stances, a social studies education that "resists narrative closure" works to cultivate "a knowing that contains within it an inescapable and profound not-knowing" (Ellsworth, 2005, p. 114). Social studies becomes, then, concerned with the status and activation of ignorance (Felman, 1982) and ultimately a working through, rather than an overcoming of, the difficulties of knowledge.

The question around which my thinking here revolves—Why didn't I know this before?—points simultaneously to various conditions of knowing and to not-knowing. Rather than attempt to answer this question, I theorize the conditions that give rise to its articulation. I begin by explaining the context in which the question was elicited. I will then move within the question by drawing from the work of Lacan (1988a, 1988b), Britzman (1998), and Felman (1991) relating pedagogy with and within crisis. Each of these authors explores crisis encountered in trauma as an inherent component of learning, thus, also engaging with key features of difficult knowledge. Finally, I will conclude the chapter and the book with a discussion of questions and their role in democracy, social studies, difficult knowledge, and psychoanalysis.

Context(s) of Inquiry

In the social studies methods courses that I teach I have frequently had students read and discuss *The Shock Doctrine*, whose thesis is that the major geopolitical events of the past 50 years were not born in freedom and motivated by democracy. Instead, *The Shock Doctrine* holds that events that precipitate social breakdown, whether natural or man-made, were used to push through anti-democratic measures fitting in with a neoliberal agenda of economic and political policy. Crises become opportunities to advance particular 'solutions' according to neoliberal agendas. Most commonly, these solutions are comprised of elements of what Milton Friedman called "economic shock therapy"—rapid privatization reforms and concurrent cuts to social spending and welfare programs. The "shock" of the shock therapy is often massive unemployment, skyrocketing food prices, and massive protest. Then, another series of shocks is needed to quell dissent. This is where the shock of fear tactics, imprisonment, and even torture becomes effective. Klein illustrates this set of practices in Argentina with the US backing of Pinochet's government, Iraq after the US invasion in 2002, post-Katrina New Orleans, post-Apartheid South Africa, and post-Cold War Poland. In each of these cases, large crowds convened in protest of neoliberal policies, and in each case such demonstrations were met by authorities with violence. In her thesis, a crisis is utilized not to invigorate democracy, as we are commonly told, but instead to implement unpopular free-market policies.

Three ideas come together to substantiate the thesis put forward in *The Shock Doctrine*. First is the idea that those in power have used that shock strategically to further cement their power and status. The second is that radical free market policies are so wildly unpopular that they can only be instituted when populations are in states of shock and presumably unable to resist. Finally, after the populations begin to resist, then the "shock" of war, imprisonment, and economic/political calamity takes effect. *The Shock Doctrine* essentially states that only through often-violent enforcement of anti-democratic processes can the kinds of changes that we often are encouraged to celebrate as free and democratic actually take place.

The radical free market project described in *The Shock Doctrine* is to place as much of the state apparatus into the hands of private companies as possible. Although the reader encounters documentation of mass protest, Klein states the fact that such policies have always been wildly unpopular, as they result in high levels of unemployment and soaring prices. The reader is asked to understand that only in a post-crisis state of shock are such policies able to be implemented:

> Take a second look at the iconic events of our era and behind many you will find [the shock doctrine's] logic at work. This is the secret history of the free market. It wasn't born in freedom and democracy. It was born in shock. (Klein & Cuaron, 2007)

The text takes the notion of shock, illustrates it as an archaic and misguided attempt at personal therapy, and makes it more frightening due to the way it was taken from the context of the clinic into the realm of political and economic policy making. There, the use of shock is deployed on the societal scale within the logics of neoliberal theory of the market. Instead of using shock therapy to take individuals into a regression such that they can be re-programmed, it is used as a moment of implementation, one that lends itself to the unpopular programs of making every service a function of markets rather than governments or public institutions.

I use the text in my social studies methods courses for several reasons. One is that it presents an alternative narrative to historical events. Alternative tellings, or multiple perspectives, are structured parts of the social studies curriculum. However, this alternative telling is not what students are used to when they think of multiple perspectives, which are most generally relatively "safe" (e.g., First Nations peoples must have thought it was bad that Europeans were here, but the Europeans must have thought it was good). *The Shock Doctrine*, on the other hand, is a complete re-organization of the events. It completely reframes the telling of the history through a different lens. The second reason for utilizing this text is that in reading it, students are invited to learn about events about which they had little or no knowledge. However, the perspective it offers also constructs a different narrative, doing something different than adding another instance that easily fits into existing narrative frameworks. For some students, then, the events seem new. Other students, though, are familiar with the geopolitical contexts of the case studies offered in *The Shock Doctrine*, but the different narratives made from them (see den Heyer & Abbott, 2011) makes familiar events strange. That is, students may have had knowledge of the events but as contextualized in starkly different plots that organize their existing narrative sense of geopolitics and history. Examples of this new content are the US support or direct involvement in the overthrow of democratically elected governments in Chile, Argentina, and Guatemala and the record of US foreign policy being often deployed in direct and conscious opposition to, rather than support of, democracy. These ideas seem curious, even troubling, to many students.

The situation of difficult knowledge is therefore staged due to the violent and traumatic ways in which these processes have been carried out, and students demonstrate a variety of reactions, as one might expect. Many students disavow Klein's thesis altogether as conspiratorial garbage, and it certainly does provide a totalizing narrative that is available for critique. Others read the text as a measured analysis of world events and a helpful framing reference to understand our current geopolitical landscape. Some others read it passively, I'm sure, as a strategy to placate the teacher and jump through the hoops of their certification programs. Despite the wide range of reactions, in my teaching of this text over several semesters one reaction that has been articulated by at least one of the students at some point during our conversation on *The Shock Doctrine*: Why did I not know this before?

What Is the "This"?

I find a complicated relationship between politics and pedagogy, crisis and learning in the question Why didn't I know this before? The question demarcates a space in which the structure of knowledge is in flux. To exemplify this process of the changing structure of knowledge I will draw on the financial crisis of 2008–2012 and how the text reconfigures dominant modes of inquiry relating to it. Every student understands that we are in the aftermath of a financial crisis. However, *The Shock Doctrine* helps students understand that such a crisis is being addressed in a way that forecloses alternative conceptions of how a society or nation would move through it. In other words, the multiple perspectives on offer, among different free-market solutions, are widened through Klein's argument. Her stance counters dominant narratives most students find familiar: More markets are better; democratic principles go hand in hand with free market principles, and the like. Furthering the thesis that the most widely circulated accounts of the financial crisis fail to address the issue from any other discursive location than from inside the logic of capital, Žižek (2009) writes, "It is as if recent events were staged with a calculated risk in order to demonstrate that, even at a time of shattering crisis, there is no viable alternative to capitalism" (p. 16). Recall that rather than protecting those to whom the greatest material risks were posed with the immediate provision of state money, the US government gave hundreds of billions of dollars to the financial corporations themselves. Thus, moments of crisis are used to further entrench the same actors, policies, and processes that gave rise to the crisis in the first place. The students reading Klein's text are confronted with the challenge of coming to terms with, what is for many, a new way of considering economic systems and the policies and ideologies that regulate them.

On an initial read, the students' question could be an acknowledgment of what is felt to be "new information." It seems apparent in the articulation of the question that there is information within Klein's work (the "this") that brings the free-market project into sharp relief in ways that reveals the connection between economic policy and social reality. Students, we might say, have added some discrete bits of content knowledge to their arsenal. In addition to being a text that helps students acquire new content knowledge, *The Shock Doctrine*, as I mentioned above, also works to re-contextualize and reframe what many students already know or have at least heard of. There are, of course, many texts that operate along a similar axis of disrupting normative conceptualizations of a host of topics (e.g., Toni Morrison's *Beloved*, Jamaica Kincaid's *A Small Place*). Each of those two texts works in relationship different narrative structures (slavery and colonialism, respectively). In the case of the *The Shock Doctrine*, Klein provides an interpretive lens that will bring critical processes of democracy, marketization, neoliberalism, and corporatism into relief. In this sense, it is not necessarily the case that the student articulating the question of knowledge is not familiar with content, it is that the particular framing and narration of the content are felt as novel and, as indicated by the simple articulation of the question, important to have said out loud, in language, or in the psychoanalytic vocabulary "symbolized." If students already knew "this," they may not have known it in this particular way. It may be, in other words, that the student has changed not what they know but how they know it (see, for elaboration on learning as difference, Ellsworth, 1997, pp. 60–61). As we pull the question back, we see that it indicates a change in the structure or emplotment, rather than the status or location, of knowledge.

Such an encounter invites a relation with difficult knowledge in both ways of thinking of the term: on the one hand because the scenes in which Klein writes are populated with violence and loss, and on the other hand because of the ways in which her account challenges the already-there narratives around which explanations of the world are set.

Moving within the Question: Figuring Crisis with Pedagogy and Learning

Put simply, in coming to terms with "the this," a student who articulates the question of knowledge may be in a struggle with accommodating what seems to be new information into old frameworks of knowing. Such an event, when read psychoanalytically, alludes to relationships between learning, crisis and trauma. For Pitt and Britzman (2003), the learning that comes from encountering representations of social and historical trauma—difficult knowledge—can instantiate a kind of crisis for the learner in that "questions of knowledge are made and broken" as old ideas are painfully confronted and as "beautiful substitutes" for that knowledge emerge (p. 761). This breaking of knowledge occurs in pedagogy when old stories are called into question as I believe is the case here as signified by the question posed by students.

Further, there is an expressed desire codified in that question that points to an indictment of the prior state of not-knowing. Their education seems to be called into question. In this sense the learning itself occurs in the trauma's wake (which is, again, the location of significance of trauma, the "afterward" of it) and manifests itself as a crisis of encountering one's existing structure of understanding as insufficient. To put this in a Lacanian way, we might say that "truth causes a collapse of knowledge" (2007, p. 186; see also Cho, 2009). Truth, for Lacan, is not a static object of knowledge, rather it is a situation that results from a new awareness of old situations that "creates a production" (Lacan, 2007, p. 186; for truth as a production or generative process, see den Heyer & Conrad, 2011). Klein's narrative may not be "the truth" as we traditional use the term, but in relation to students' allusion to the insufficiency of their prior understanding, it may function as a Lacanian truth. The encounter is productive in that understanding might be differently structured; already known facts/events become 'new' as one's relationship to their previously taken for granted meanings change. Thus, we are presented with a theory of learning where history (personal, as in psychoanalysis, and social, as in social studies education) is made present through these processes of collapse and confrontation between old and new ways of experiencing and articulating what counts as knowledge and to know.

It is possible that what the students knew before as "history" is undergoing the kind of revision that psychoanalytic theory would refer to as deferred knowledge or "the revision of experiences, memories, and impressions [that] are made to fit new circumstances" (Britzman, 2000, p. 30; see also Britzman, 2003). However, they might also be confronting a version of a "before" that lacks, at least immediately, a prior context. What a learner encounters upon their exposure to *The Shock Doctrine*, then, is not just another history lesson. It is the lesson of another history altogether, one that places the events into a context provided by violence, not peace, and imposition rather than democracy. It may be that such learning is jarring due to the preponderance of messages that promote a narrative framing of Western democracies as being promoters of peace, democracy and justice. The learner, like the citizen, is subjected to the inadequacy of dominant discourses and indeed the inadequacy of language itself experienced with the necessity to make new meanings possible through the alternative narrative framing of the familiar. The world, in this moment, in this particular pedagogical interactions, is not what the learner thought it was, and learners are compelled to ask, "Why didn't I know this before?" Quick on the heels of this is another question that may follow, "What am I supposed to 'do' with this knowledge (if) experienced as a potentially productive awareness."

Learning as Crisis in the Multiplying of Perspective

Psychoanalytic thinking may help us think productively about the terrain around this question. In psychoanalysis learning is constituted "with the curious ways in which ideas and affect organize and reorganize each other and attach themselves to new experiences" (Pitt, 1998, p. 541). Many students react to Klein's thesis with disbelief, denial, and shock. Why did I not know this before? Is this true? If this is true, then what else that I don't know is true? What else is going on? What am I supposed to do about/with this? What now? Such questions point us to the student confronting his or her own ignorance requiring both a recognition and reorganization of his or her history of knowledge. The student recognizes the absence of knowledge and then reorganizes the history in such a way as to condemn the same absence. Such questions indicate a relationship between trauma, pedagogy, crisis, and knowledge that Felman (1991) has theorized as being a crucial pedagogical moment.

Crisis involves something of a profound recognition of a shift in subjectivity or experience without which the pedagogical act seems to lack efficacy, as I elaborated in chapter two. Felman (1991) presents us with a fundamental need for the instantiation of crisis in order to do any true pedagogical work. While the *Shock Doctrine* is an indictment of the manipulating of crisis and the uses of mass social trauma, Felman requires us to rotate our vantage point on crisis. Crisis now takes on a crucial pedagogical dimension and allows us to see the student crisis not only as disruptive and perhaps felt to be dangerous or risky but also as the prerequisite to the work of learning, the work of re-symbolizing.

Here, then, read more psychoanalytically, the question of "Why didn't I know this before?" indicts my own knowledge, implicates my self, and within the query places its indictment on the "I" instead of the "this"—my worldview, my experiences, rather than the text or the messenger. The question is indicative that the force of turning focus back on a personal history in which what structured my knowledge is no longer adequate. Learning about crisis has hit upon yet another crisis, this time one in which the learner has no prior context in which to articulate or accommodate what it is that they are expected to learn other than the earliest of contexts; contexts where the radically dependent infant feels the pushes and pulls of helplessness (Farley, 2009) and fulfillment in a world not of his or her own making.

If we are expected to learn anything about the world, Felman (1991) teaches, we had better be prepared for the injuries that this learning might inflict. She writes:

> To seek reality is both to set out to explore the injury inflicted by it—to turn back on, and to try to penetrate, the state of being stricken, wounded by reality—and to attempt, at the same time, to reemerge from the paralysis of the state, to engage reality as an advent, a movement, and as a vital, critical necessity of moving on. It is beyond the shock of being stricken, but nonetheless within the wound and from within the woundedness that the event, incomprehensible though it may be, becomes accessible. (p. 28)

Here we are asked by Felman to take the experience of being stricken by crisis as the object of inquiry, folding experience back onto itself in the hope of moving through modalities of understanding about the nature of the crisis itself. In the moments of that encounter with what Felman here is calling "reality," we are encouraged to recognize the ways in which we are made to feel paralyzed by it and to think about that moment as a moment of possibility. Such a stance helps me wonder about the degree to which students asking "Why didn't I know this before?" indicates the status of this particular engagement.

Multiplying Perspectives in Social Studies Education

Lacan (1988b) acknowledged the ways that the very process of learning is a process of reconstituting what was known before:

> When something comes to light, something which we are forced to consider as new, when another structural order emerges…it creates its own perspective within the past and we say—This can never not have been there, this has existed from the beginning. (p. 5)

What Lacan is discussing is not dissimilar from what occurs when multiple perspectives are introduced in social studies. This chapter is about a time when for some students something new has come to the light of their attention. "Why didn't I know this before?" becomes a trace of that other structural order where the status of knowledge before the encounter is now rendered differently. It is now deficient, indicted. Thus, knowledge has been deferred.

What these considerations imply for social studies teachers is a consideration of the loose and nonlinear chronology of learning and knowledge combined with the dynamic nature of historical work and the manner in which students attach meaning to that work. In this process of deferred knowledge, the experience, a memory, comes to take new meaning in our lives. The psychoanalytic stance toward history privileges the reworking of our historical narrative. In this sense through, the psychoanalytic idea of deferred action, history changes so that we, too, can change. It is, then, a position that includes the possibility for difference.

Knowing that students will in many pedagogical instances encounter and necessarily move within and through a crisis need not necessarily make the pedagogue a sadist whose focus is on producing crisis for its own sake. Rather, the pedagogical implication of taking Felman (1991) seriously is to understand that in enacting a responsible pedagogy we ought to expect (though not force) students to encounter various states of crisis. This should be so particularly in social studies classrooms where so much of the content consists of potentially traumatic knowledge. When a student asks "Why didn't I know this before?"

in response to reading *The Shock Doctrine*, their past knowledge is indicted as having always been flawed or incomplete, but that history of learning is only constituted in the very moment of learning articulated by that question. This represents and signifies the dynamic of the relation of difficult knowledge.

Neither content nor pedagogy was at issue in the question students pose. Rather, the issue was about the ways in which the content was activated not only in a pedagogical relation but also in a psychical relation with an already existing structure of knowledge. What taught, what gave the eliciting motivation to the question, was something about which I am speculating. But in that speculation, I hope, is a productive way of looking and listening, of an attunement to the ways that students understand their relationships between each other, their students, and within the world. And as a social studies educator, that relationship between self and other and the ways that knowledge structures that relationship remains of primary concern.

Conclusion: Going without Answers

Imagine a class scenario in which questions were supposed to be met with answers, and a student asked the question, "Why didn't I know this before"? A teacher could respond coyly by saying that they did not know this before because it hadn't been taught to them before. Another answer could be a prolonged engagement with the idea of implicit and null curriculum and the political terrain of the social studies curriculum. This would be worthy of exploration, I think. Yet, in my view, there is something else to be done with questions aside from answering them at all. Instead, perhaps the question can simply be returned to the student as another inquiry about the location from whence the question arose. As I've stated throughout this book, a fundamental assertion that difficult knowledge will make into conversations about social studies is that the pedagogical encounter ought to be considered as an extended, prolonged engagement in which inquiry is left open more often than it is closed. When multiple perspectives are introduced, competing claims are made that fit into competing narratives that simply cannot be reconciled due to the ways in which this competition will forcefully benefit only a particular group or groups. Such a conflict inevitably provokes questions.

"It is as though," Adam Phillips (2004) writes, "Psychoanalysts are people who have discovered something about answering that makes them suspicious." So what is it that questions do, and why is it that they seem to do more than point us toward an answer? Social studies educators themselves have focused on questions as having considerable significance. The C3 framework (NCSS, 2013) centers questions as foundational to the projects of inquiry that yield what they call understanding—the initiating genre of inquiry that frames the entire curriculum. Questions begin the entire process and, thus, are critical to social studies. But what if one decided that answering the questions took a different valence than a disciplined understanding? The C3 framework orients a pedagogy that assumes understanding can be achieved through disciplinary strategies:

> Understanding is achieved by the careful investigation of questions, data collection, reading, analysis, and synthesis; in effect, data are transformed into evidence-based claims that separate opinions and conjecture from justifiable understandings. (p. 89)

The pedagogy here begins with a question and ends with achieved understanding. Recalling the ways in which data, analysis, and claim making are all going to entail emotional and ambiguous work, it seems as though understanding ought to include an additional facet of work which is a reflexive and self-conscious acknowledgment of our own partiality. I am a strong advocate for the analysis of evidence, aiding students in their ability to delineate the difference between justifiable claims and wild conjecture. These things have enormous consequences. And that is why something crucial like understanding ought not be considered "achieved" at any point.

It is worth noting Lacan's (1998a) warning about the care with which an analyst must approach her or his work, in saying "to interpret and to imagine one understands are not at all the same. It is precisely the opposite" (p. 73). What Lacan is referencing in this statement is that suspicion of answers. Understanding poses as a final resting place when our attachments to, or discomforts with, our ways of thinking about the world are pushed and pulled in many directions.

In psychoanalysis we are asked to consider questions that cannot be answered, only extended, to prolong the encounter with a problem. If we can continue to remain within the question, then we can continue to look for resources for ongoing understanding, and it means that we have the chance to continue learning. I can ask the question where the answer is not one that forecloses inquiry. Rather, it prompts me to think again about the nature of classroom life and the lives that people make there. One of the pedagogical benefits of psychoanalysis is, I think, is in its refusal to provide a how-to manual (Britzman, 2011), to analysis, to teaching, to living life in general.

What is it to teach, what is to be taught, if we are not going to be told what to do or what to think? Britzman's (2011) refusal to offer certainty or prescription centers the impossibility of certainty in pedagogical contexts in that "any desire for certainty could mean only that something was terribly uncertain" (p. 83). She extends this axiom to include a questioning of the educator's desire or thought that she or he knows what is best for a student, or that he or she knows what will come of the educational scene at all. It means that we can acknowledge that learning about the world is so often bewildering when we think about the world as being replete with catastrophe on both a large and small scale.

Democracy requires a lot of people who are capable and willing to do the hard work of being together and participating in ways that are mutually beneficial though always marked by compromise. Social studies education, our interests in learning to be with others in the world, is not at any point a final achievement. The procedural unfolding of a democracy requiring invested actors is not a difficult idea. Yet the unfolding itself will require, it seems, the relation of difficult knowledge. We will have to face the devastation that marks our past and present. We will have to confront the idea that education will not come with a guarantee that what we learn will make us happy. We will have to hold competing thoughts in mind without reaching for a final answer between, say, our working with students on their critical reading of evidence and, on the other hand, knowing that evidence is often a weak intervention into thinking. This does not mean throwing out the evidence. What it does mean is making sure that we recognize the difficult complexities of social studies education because of the high stakes of such learning. It might mean asking students to study the ways that, because we are human, we resist learning, and how learning might itself require resistance to begin.

When considering the biggest issues of our time—climate change, mass migration, inequitable wealth distribution, the ramification of hyper-connection, social media, and surveillance, and the like—it is likely that we will become overwhelmed. Learning about the big picture requires us to ask questions about how we will relate to the world in a way that allows us to carry on and find creative ways to navigate these complicated systems. Learning is the situation in which a new vantage, a multiple perspective, is offered on what we thought we were able to recognize but now seems unfamiliar. Multiple perspectives offer novel vantages and precipitate questions, questions about difficult knowledge that we probably never asked for but also that we cannot do without. They are necessary for the hard affiliative, relational, and intimate work of democracy and world building.

When people wonder why they did not know something before, it indicates a measure of worthiness of that knowledge under consideration but an unworthiness of the status of a prior ignorance. Such dynamic pushes and pulls mark the relation of difficult knowledge. They are the result of a social studies education that asks students and teachers to engage in thinking about the world as a dynamic place in which we make all kinds of choices and all kinds of lives.

Social studies education is heavily populated with definitions and delineations about the varied approaches, goals, and outcomes that can, do, or ought to occur within it. Further explorations are needed about the ways in which difficult knowledge is a pedagogical relation among teachers, learners, and a world that is populated with all kinds of things about which we would rather not know. Difficult knowledge in that sense is about how the social world is risky and how learning about that risk can bring the learner in relation to profound instances of suffering and loss. Difficult knowledge brings our vulnerability to the fore of the pedagogical scene as we encounter the traumas of others, and we navigate the crisis made from such an encounter.

References

Britzman, D. P., (1998). *Lost subjects, contested objects: Toward a psychoanalytic inquiry of learning.* Albany, NY: SUNY Press.

Britzman, D. P. (2000). Teacher education in the confusion of our times. *Journal of Teacher Education, 51* (3), 200–205.

Britzman, D. P. (2003). *After-education: Anna Freud, Melanie Klein, and psychoanalytic histories of learning.* Albany, NY: SUNY Press.

Britzman, D.P. (2009). *The very thought of education: Psychoanalysis and the impossible professions.* Albany, NY. SUNY Press.

Britzman, D.P. (2011). *Freud and education.* New York, NY: Routledge.

Cho, K.D. (2009). *Psychopedagogy: Freud, Lacan and the psychoanalytic theory of education.* New York, NY: Palgrave Macmillan.

den Heyer, K. & Abbott, L. (2011). Reverberating echoes: Challenging teacher candidates to tell and learn from entwined narrations of Canadian history. *Curriculum Inquiry, 41* (5), 610–635.

den Heyer, K. & Conrad, D. (2011). Using Alain Badiou's ethic of truths to support an 'eventful' social justice teacher education program. *Journal of Curriculum Theorizing, 27* (1), 7–19.

Ellsworth, E. A. (1997). *Teaching positions: Difference, pedagogy, and the power of address.* New York, NY: Teachers College Press.

Ellsworth, E. A. (2005) *Places of learning: Media, architecture, pedagogy.* New York, NY: Routledge.

Farley, L. (2009). Radical hope: or, the problem of uncertainty in history education. *Curriculum Inquiry, 39* (4), 537–554.

Felman, S. (1982). Psychoanalysis and education: Teaching terminable and interminable. *Yale French Studies* (63), 21–44.

Felman, S. (1987). *Jacques Lacan and the adventure of insight: Psychoanalysis in contemporary culture.* Cambridge, MA: Harvard University Press.

Felman, S. (1991). Education and crisis, or the vicissitudes of teaching. *American Imago, 48* (1), 13–73.

Kincheloe, J. (2001). *Getting beyond the facts: Teaching social studies/social sciences in the twenty-first century.* New York, NY: Peter Lang.

Klein, N. (2008). *The shock doctrine: The rise of disaster capitalism.* New York, NY: Metropolitan Books.

Klein, N. & Cuaron, A. (2007). *The shock doctrine: The rise of disaster capitalism.* Short film retrieved from http://www.youtube.com/watch?v=aSF0e6oO_tw

Lacan, J. (1988a). *The seminar of Jacques Lacan, Book I: Freud's papers on technique, 1953–1954* (1st American ed.). New York, NY: W.W. Norton.

Lacan, J. (1988b). *The seminar of Jacques Lacan Book II: The ego in Freud's theory and in the technique of psychoanalysis, 1954–1955.* New York, NY: W.W. Norton.

Lacan, J. (2007). *The seminar of Jacques Lacan, Book XVII: The other side of psychoanalysis.* New York, NY: W. W. Norton.

Matthews, S. (2009). Hitler's car as curriculum text: Reading adolescents reading history. *Journal of the Canadian Association for Curriculum Studies, 7* (2), 49–85.

National Council for the Social Studies (NCSS). (2013). *The college, career, and civic life (C3) framework for social studies state standards: Guidance for enhancing the rigor of k-12 civics, economics, geography, and history* (Silver Spring, MD: NCSS).

Pitt, A. J. (1998). Qualifying resistance: Some comments on methodological dilemmas. *International Journal of Qualitative Studies in Education, 11* (4), 535–553

Pitt, A.J., & Britzman, D. P. (2003). Speculations on qualities of difficult knowledge in teaching and learning: An experiment in psychoanalytic research. *International Journal of Qualitative Studies in Education, 16*(6), 755–776.

Phillips, A. (2004). Psychoanalysis as education. *Psychoanalytic Review, 91*(6), 779–799.

Segall, A. (2006). What's the purpose of teaching a discipline anyway? The case of history. In A. Segall, E. Heilman & C. Cherryholmes (Eds.), *Social studies—the next generation: Researching in the postmodern.* (pp. 125–139). New York, NY: Peter Lang.

Seixas, P. (2001). Schweigen! Die Kinder! Or, does postmodern history have a place in the schools? In P. N. Stearns & P. Seixas (Eds.), *Knowing, teaching and learning history: National and international perspectives.* (pp. 19–37). New York, NY:New York University Press.

White, H. (2001). Emplotment and the problem of truth. In G. Roberts (Ed.), *The history and narrative reader.* (pp. 375–389). New York: Routledge.

Wineburg, S. S. (2001). *Historical thinking and other unnatural acts: Charting the future of teaching the past.* Philadelphia, PA: Temple University Press.

Žižek, S. (2009). *First as tragedy, then as farce.* Brooklyn, NY: Verso.

INDEX

Studies in Criticality

General Editor
Shirley R. Steinberg

Counterpoints publishes the most compelling and imaginative books being written in education today. Grounded on the theoretical advances in criticalism, feminism, and postmodernism in the last two decades of the twentieth century, Counterpoints engages the meaning of these innovations in various forms of educational expression. Committed to the proposition that theoretical literature should be accessible to a variety of audiences, the series insists that its authors avoid esoteric and jargonistic languages that transform educational scholarship into an elite discourse for the initiated. Scholarly work matters only to the degree it affects consciousness and practice at multiple sites. Counterpoints' editorial policy is based on these principles and the ability of scholars to break new ground, to open new conversations, to go where educators have never gone before.

For additional information about this series or for the submission of manuscripts, please contact:

Shirley R. Steinberg
c/o Peter Lang Publishing, Inc.
29 Broadway, 18th floor
New York, New York 10006

To order other books in this series, please contact our Customer Service Department:

(800) 770-LANG (within the U.S.)
(212) 647-7706 (outside the U.S.)
(212) 647-7707 FAX

Or browse online by series:
www.peterlang.com